Susan L. Lingo

Fold-N-Hold

Object Talks for Kids!

Standard
PUBLISHING
CINCINNATI, OHIO

Dedication

How great is the love the Father has lavished on us,
that we should be called children of God! And that is what we are!
1 John 3:1

Fold-n-Hold Object Talks for Kids
© 2004 by Susan L. Lingo

Published by Standard Publishing Company, Cincinnati, Ohio 45231. A division of Standex International Corporation.

Credits
Produced by Susan L. Lingo, Bright Ideas Books™
Illustrated by Marilynn G. Barr
Cover design by Diana Walters

10 09 08 07 06 05 04   7 6 5 4 3 2 1
ISBN 0-7847-1603-X
Printed in the United States of America

Contents

The Miraculous Catch

Cool 3-D fish remind kids that Jesus' provision is perfect!

Luke 5:4-6; Philippians 4:19

Simple Supplies

✦ 8-inch square paper
✦ black markers
✦ scissors, tape
✦ construction paper
✦ thread or fishing line

Before Class

Collect your craft supplies and follow the directions for making the fish in the diagrams from this activity. Fold several fish and tape varying lengths of fishing line to them. Tape the other ends of the line from a rolled paper pole. Kids will make two or three fish and add verses to them during the object talk.

The Fold-n-Hold Message

Ask kids if there was ever a time they needed something very much but weren't sure how to get what was needed or from whom. Encourage kids to tell how it felt to be in need and what it was like when their needs were finally met. Say: **There are times when we need things so much that it takes up our whole focus. Perhaps we're sick and need a special medicine to feel better. Maybe we're hungry and can't find food or it's raining and we need shelter. Perhaps we just need an encouraging word or to feel loved and treasured. When we have needs, we need them to be met. But by whom?**

Hold up your fishing line and paper fish. Say: **This big catch of fish reminds me of a time when Jesus' disciples needed something and how Jesus provided for their needs—and much more! Let's fold some awesome paper fish as we discover more about our needs and how Jesus meets them perfectly every time. Before folding our fish, we have a few needs of our own! We need paper, markers, and scissors.**

Demonstrate the following step-by-step directions using the diagrams. Make sure kids complete each step before moving on. Allow friends to help if needed.

Step 1. Fold the paper into a triangle. Then fold the top corners to meet at the bottom center.

Step 2. Fold the flaps you just finished from the center bottom up to meet at the center top.

Step 3. Fold the flaps back diagonally.

Step 4. (a) Fold one of the lower flaps up to the center of the triangle. (b) Then fold it up to even off the lower edge. Flip the fish over and fold up the lower flap even with the bottom.

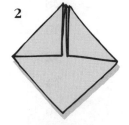

1

2

3

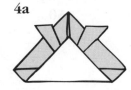

4a

Step 5. Open and puff out the fish from the bottom edge, then bring the sides together and press down to flatten.

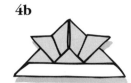

4b

Step 6. Trim away the top and bottom corners, then flip the two tail fins outward, and you're done!

When the fish are folded, have kids roll fishing poles from construction paper. Cut lengths of fishing line and tape one end to the fish and the other ends to the ends of the poles. When the fishing poles are completed, read aloud Luke 5:4-6, then ask:

5

✦ *What did Jesus' disciples need?*
✦ *How did Jesus supply their needs and help them?*
✦ *How do you think the disciples felt after Jesus provided for them in such a miraculous way?*
✦ *In what ways has Jesus provided for you in your life?*

Say: **Our needs are as many and as varied as there are people. But whether a need is for food, clothing, help, healing, encouragement, hope, or love, we all share common needs for forgiveness of our sins and for salvation so we can live with God someday! Jesus can supply every need we have at the right time and in the right way. Listen to what else God's Word tells us about Jesus' provision.** Read aloud Philippians 4:19. Ask:

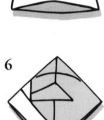

6

✦ *How does God provide for us through Jesus?*
✦ *When Jesus supplies for our needs, in what ways is God also supplying for our needs?*
✦ *Is there any need that Jesus cannot provide for? Explain.*

Say: **God gave Jesus all authority here on earth, and that includes the power and authority to help us by providing for our needs. Because Jesus loves us and listens to our prayers and requests, He promises to answer through His help. There is no need too large or small for Jesus to provide for in His perfect ways and time. Think of two or three needs you have right now today, such as healing for a sick friend or family member, help with school or another worry, or something personal in your life such as patience or forgiveness. Then write those needs on your paper fish using a marker. Then hang your miraculous catch of fish in your room at home and pray for those needs each night. You'll be surprised at how powerfully and perfectly Jesus will supply for your needs!**

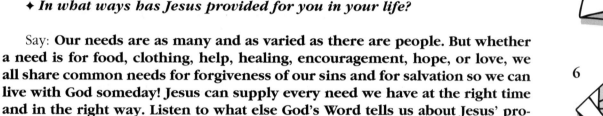

If there's time, have kids each fold two more fish. Place small paper clips on the fish and make a fishing pole from rolled and taped paper. Tie a small magnet on the end of the fishing-pole line. Let kids take turns "fishing." Each time a fish is caught, have kids name one need that Jesus can meet in our lives or repeat a memory verse they're working on!

Lost & Found Lamb

These super simple lambs remind kids that God wants us close to Him!

Luke 15:4-7; 19:10

Simple Supplies

- 8-inch squares of white paper
- wiggly eyes
- craft glue
- black markers

Before Class

Collect the materials needed and make a lamb or two to become familiar with the simple folding techniques. (Hint: Sample squares of white embossed wallpaper make the lambs even more sturdy and tactile!)

The Fold-n-Hold Message

Invite kids to share about times they may have lost something special or valuable and how it felt. Encourage kids to tell what it was like when their special items were finally found. Then say: **It feels awful to lose something of great value, doesn't it? You want that treasure close to you and feel lost without it! Imagine how God feels when one of His precious people wanders about through disobedience, wrong choices, or angry thoughts. God doesn't want us to be lost from Him— He wants us close to Him! There's a story Jesus told in the book of Luke about a lost sheep and how important that one sheep was to the shepherd. Let's do a bit of paper folding as we discover why that sheep was so important.**

Distribute the squares of white paper. Then slowly demonstrate the following step-by-step folding directions using the diagrams. Make sure that kids complete each simple-to-fold step before moving on.

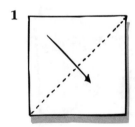

Step 1. Fold the paper square into a triangle. (Tell kids how one of a shepherd's 99 sheep was lost.)

Step 2. Fold two of the corners in toward the center to make "ears." (Tell kids that the shepherd looked everywhere—even under bushes and rocks. Lift the ear flaps to peek under them.)

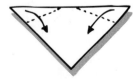

Step 3. Fold the two corner points of the ears inward.

Step 4. Color in a nose and glue on wiggly eyes. (Explain how happy the shepherd was when his lost lamb was found.)

When the paper lambs are folded, say: The shepherd was so sad when he saw that one of his precious lambs was lost! He was frantic and immediately left his flock to go and search for that one lamb. Ask:

+ *Why was one lamb important when the shepherd had so many others?*
+ *Do you think the shepherd would ever give up looking for his sheep? Explain.*
+ *In what ways is this how God looks for us if we become lost from Him?*

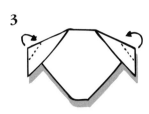

Say: **Jesus told this parable of the Lost Sheep to explain how important each of us is to God. Jesus wanted us to know that God desires us to stay close to Him and that, if we wander away, He will bring us back. Think for a moment about the shepherd who loved his sheep and about the lost lamb.** Ask:

+ *How is Jesus like that shepherd who loved his sheep so greatly?*
+ *In what ways are we like Jesus' sheep who sometimes wander away from Him?*
+ *Why do you think there's so much rejoicing in heaven when a sinner who is lost from God is found and stays close to God?*
+ *In what ways did Jesus come to seek and save people?*

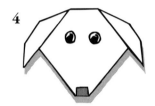

Read aloud Luke 19:10, then have kids use markers to write the verse on the backs of their paper sheep. When the verse is written, have kids read it in unison. Then say: **God wants us to stay close to Him all the time. That's why God sent Jesus! Jesus helps us stay—and not stray from—being close to God. Remember: God never wanders away from us—it's we who wander away from God. And God feels great sadness if we wander from Him! What are ways we can stay close to God all the time?** Invite kids to share their ideas, which might include learning God's Word, reading the Bible, praying, and serving God and others.

If there's time, form two groups and have one group hide their eyes while the other group hides their paper sheep in the room. Let kids search for the lost lambs. When all are found, shout: "What was lost is now found!" Then let the groups switch hide-and-seek roles.

Kids may enjoy embellishing their paper lambs by gluing cotton balls to the ears. Make a whole flock of folded sheep and attach them to a bulletin board with the caption: "Stay—Don't Stray!" You might wish to use these folded sheep to discuss Isaiah 53:6 with kids and relate the concept of going "astray" with wandering from God in sin and how Jesus saved us.

Leap of Faith!

Cute frogs teach kids that faith doesn't sit still.

James 2:17

Simple Supplies

◆ 8-inch squares of green or yellow paper
◆ markers, scissors
◆ eye stickers or wiggly eyes
◆ craft glue

Before Class

Make one or two of these cute, hoppity frogs so you're familiar with the folding instructions and how to make them "leap." Consider drawing a pattern for the 8-inch square and then photocopying it on green or yellow construction paper or card stock. Let kids cut out the squares just prior to this message.

The Fold-n-Hold Message

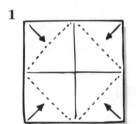

Place the squares of paper across the center of the floor and gather kids on one side of the papers. Tell kids that the squares represent temptations, worries, or other troublesome concerns in our lives. Ask kids to tell what some of those worries or troubles might include, such as telling lies to parents or teachers, being unkind to friends, gossiping, cheating, or temptations to make wrong decisions.

Say: **We all have times and situations in our lives that cause us so much worry or trouble that we're not sure what to do about them. How do we get over these troublesome spots in our lives? How can we get over these paper squares? We make a giant leap!** Lead kids in leaping over the paper squares, then say: **Just as giant leaps sent us over the papers, leaps of faith can help us trust God and get to the other side of troubles! Let's fold some lively, leaping frogs from paper as we discover more about what a leap of faith—and trusting God—can do for us.**

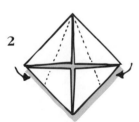

Have kids pick up the paper squares, then demonstrate the following step-by-step folding directions for making paper frogs. Be sure kids complete each step before moving on. Allow friends to help if needed.

Step 1. Fold a paper square in half, then in half once more. Crease the folds well, then open up the square and spread it flat.

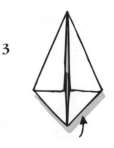

Steps 2 & 3. Fold each of the four corners to the center point. Then fold each of the two top edges to the center line.

Step 4. Fold the triangle at the bottom upward.

Step 5. Fold each of the bottom corners to the center of the bottom edge. Then fold the bottom portion upward.

Step 6. Fold the top half of the lower rectangle downward toward yourself. This forms the frog's "legs."

Step 7. Give the frog a head by folding the tip of the upper point downward. Add two eyes and draw an "X" toward the back of the frog.

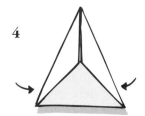

When the paper frogs are finished, show kids how to make their frogs "leap" by gently pushing down on the letter X, then sliding their fingers back and away from the frogs. Say: **When we have troubles and worries, they often keep us stuck in poor choices and wrong behavior. But when we trust God and take a leap of faith** (flick your frog to make it hop), **we put our faith into action and can move ahead!** Invite a volunteer to read aloud James 2:17, then ask:

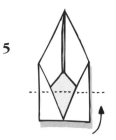

- ✦ *Why do we become "stuck" in sin or disobedience?*
- ✦ *What happens if we don't change our ways and move ahead toward God?*
- ✦ *In what ways does trusting God help us take leaps of faith to break bad behaviors or help us with troubles?*
- ✦ *How can we trust God more so leaps of faith come easier for us?*

Say: **Becoming stuck and motionless in our disobedience, troubles, and worries causes us to stop moving toward God—and that's not good! But trusting in God and taking leaps of faith can help us hop away from negative behaviors and troubles and set us on the path to following God again.**

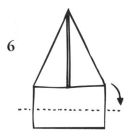

Go around the room and have kids each tell one way they can trust God or take a leap of faith this week, then have them make their frogs leap ahead. If there's time, place tape across the floor and have a leap-frog race. For extra fun, place paper-plate "lily pads" across the floor and hop from one pad to the next, counting the number of leaps to get to each.

Whale of a Prayer

Whopping whales remind kids of the importance of prayer.

Ephesians 6:18; 1 Thessalonians 5:17, 18

Simple Supplies

+ 8-inch squares of colored paper
+ scissors
+ fine-tipped markers

Before Class

Fold several big fish or whales to become familiar with the simple folding directions. Have scissors on hand for kids to make a simple snip while folding their whales.

The Fold-n-Hold Message

Invite kids to tell about times they've prayed or to repeat prayers they might say before meals or bedtime. Then ask kids if they think God really does hear and answer our prayers. Encourage kids to explain their answers.

Allow time for kids to answer, then say: **Prayer is such a powerful tool to bring us closer to God! It's true that God knows our prayers before we even pray them and our needs before we know them. But God wants us to humble ourselves and come to Him in prayer. Prayer allows us to open our hearts and recognize our need for God's help—that we can't do everything by ourselves. Jonah learned about the power of prayer when he was swallowed by the big fish.**

Invite volunteers to recount the story of Jonah and the great fish using the paper whale you folded earlier. Then say: **Jonah learned a whale of a lesson in that giant fish, and we can learn the same lessons today! Let's fold fun paper whales as we discover more about the power of prayer and what it can do in our lives.**

Hand out the paper squares, then demonstrate the following step-by-step folding directions using the diagrams. Make sure that kids complete each step before moving on. Allow friends to help if needed.

1
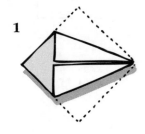

2
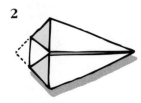

3

Step 1. Fold the square in half, then open it. Fold opposite corners of the square so that they meet at the center fold line. (Be sure there's a small triangle at the bottom of where the edges meet.)

Step 2. Fold the tip of the small triangle in so the point just touches where the corners met in the center.

Step 3. Fold the piece in half on the center fold line, folding the flaps to the inside.

Step 4. Fold the pointed end upward to make the whale's "tail."

Step 5. Make a short snip downward through the tip of the fold in the tail. Fold the two pieces of the tail outward. Use markers to add eyes and side fins (or even a smile, if you want).

When the whales are folded, say: **Wow! Just imagine being swallowed up by a giant fish! Jonah must have been afraid, worried, and very sorry that he had disobeyed God. Jonah prayed to tell God he was sorry. He prayed to ask God to forgive him. And he prayed to have hope that somehow God would save him. God heard every word of Jonah's prayers and answered in a powerful way.** Ask:

- *Do you think God would have saved Jonah if Jonah hadn't prayed for God's forgiveness? Explain.*
- *How did praying bring Jonah closer to God? How does praying bring us closer to God?*
- *Why do you think God listens to every one of our prayers?*
- *Does God always answer our prayers? How do you know?*
- *Does God always answer the way we want Him to or in the time we want Him to? Explain.*

Invite volunteers to read aloud Ephesians 6:18 and 1 Thessalonians 5:17, 18. Then say: **God's Word teaches us to pray all the time and to give thanks for God's answers no matter what. In prayer, we can tell God everything we feel, hope, dream, need, and want. And we have God's own assurance that He will listen and answer.** Read aloud Isaiah 58:9a, then say: **The power of prayer is God's power—and God offers it to you when you seek Him through your prayers!**

Let kids use markers to write Isaiah 58:9a or 1 Thessalonians 5:17 on their paper whales as reminders of the power of prayer.

Crowned Royalty

Wearable crowns remind us that Jesus is King and we're His royal kids!

Romans 8:16, 17; Philippians 2:10, 11; 1 Peter 2:9

Simple Supplies

+ 16-inch paper squares
+ markers
+ craft glue (optional)
+ plastic jewels (optional)

Before Class

Fold a paper crown and wear it as you introduce this object talk. For a really neat effect, embellish the crown with plastic jewels. Consider using rolls of shiny wrapping paper for the paper squares. If you have younger kids, you may want to use 12- or 14-inch paper squares.

The Fold-n-Hold Message

1

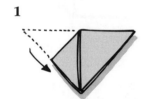

Ask kids to describe what you're wearing on your head and what a crown signifies. Then say: **In some countries, kings and queens wear special crowns to signify their royalty. They want others to recognize them as rulers and as royalty. But there was one King who didn't need an earthly crown to show His royalty. His power, wisdom, and grace to rule weren't demonstrated by a crown of gold or silver—they were demonstrated in His love! Do you know who this King of kings was?**

Allow kids to share their ideas, then say: **Jesus is our King of all kings on heaven and earth! And because we love and accept Jesus as our Savior, we have become kids of the King! Let's fold cool crowns to remind us of Jesus' royalty as we explore how Jesus rules and how we're the King's kids.**

2

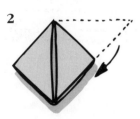

Demonstrate the following step-by-step folding directions for paper crowns using the diagrams. Make sure that kids complete each step before moving on. Invite kids to help one another if needed.

Step 1. Fold a large paper square into a triangle, then lay the triangle on a flat surface with the longest side facing away from you and largest point pointing toward you.

Step 2. Fold one of the top corners over so that it touches the bottom point. Repeat this step with the other top corner.

3

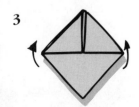

Step 3. Fold the top layer of bottom points straight upward so they meet at the top. (These are the upper tips.)

Step 4. Fold each of the upper tips over and out slightly to the sides. Crease the folds well! (There should be two triangle shapes, one on top of the other, at the bottom of the crown.)

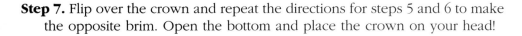

Step 5. Fold the top triangle upward over the top half of the crown so it nearly reaches the top. (There will be a small portion remaining below the center fold line.)

4

Step 6. Fold the remaining small portion upward to make the "brim" of the crown.

Step 7. Flip over the crown and repeat the directions for steps 5 and 6 to make the opposite brim. Open the bottom and place the crown on your head!

5

Kids may enjoy decorating their paper crowns with markers and plastic jewels. When the crowns are finished, let kids model them for one another. Then say: **These fun crowns are good reminders of Jesus' royalty with God as His Father. But Jesus didn't need a shiny crown to wear to demonstrate His kingship—He showed His power and wisdom through His forgiveness, love, and miraculous power to help and heal. Some people call Jesus "King," and others call Him "Lord," but however you call on the name of Jesus, there's great power in His name!** Read aloud Philippians 2:10, 11 then ask:

6

+ *Why is there such awesome power when we call upon the name of Jesus?*
+ *In what ways does confessing that Jesus is our Lord show others whom we serve and choose to follow?*
+ *How does it help us when we call upon the name of Jesus in prayer?*
+ *In what ways does acknowledging Jesus as King and Lord help us remember our role as His servants who love, follow, and serve Him?*

Say: **Jesus received His power and authority from God, and He is our Lord of lords and King of kings! And as His followers who love and acknowledge His heavenly kingship, we become His chosen people—His children!** Read aloud Romans 8:16, 17 and 1 Peter 2:9, then ask kids to tell how it feels to be loved and treasured by our Lord. Remind kids that there's great power in calling on the name of Jesus our Lord and King in prayer. Close by having kids use fine-tipped markers to write Philippians 2:10, 11 on their crowns.

Special Delivery

Fun-to-fold envelopes help kids share the Good News about Jesus.

Matthew 28:19, 20

Simple Supplies

+ colored copy paper
+ scissors
+ self-adhesive stickers
+ small index cards
+ pens or pencils
+ the envelope pattern from page 54

Before Class

Photocopy the envelope pattern from page 54 on brightly colored copy paper. Make at least one copy for each person plus a few extras for samples. Fold an envelope or two to become familiar with the simple folding techniques.

The Fold-n-Hold Message

Invite kids to tell about times they sent a special letter, greeting card, or other message to someone. Encourage kids to explain why the message was important and how it felt to be the messenger.

Say: **There are so many times we carry news, greetings, or information to others. Those messages might contain something fun, such as a birthday greeting, or they may be invitations to a special celebration—or they may even be warnings to steer clear of troubles or be important information on an illness or medicines. Whatever the messages might be, it's good to know we can be counted on to deliver them. Let's fold some special-delivery envelopes as we discover what the most important message we'll ever deliver is and why.**

Distribute the pattern pages and scissors. Demonstrate the following step-by-step folding directions using the diagrams. Make sure that kids complete each step before moving on. Allow friends to help if needed.

Step 1. Have kids cut out the patterns on the solid, outlined edges.

Step 2. Place the square on a table face up. Fold the left and right points in to meet at the center. Crease the folds well.

Step 3. Fold the lower triangle upward on the dotted line.

Step 4. Fold the edges beside the lower triangle you just folded inward and the bottom tip of the envelope upward.

Step 5. Fold the lower portion of the envelope upward (on the dotted line) to touch the center dot, then fold the top portion downward on the dotted line to make the envelope's flap.

1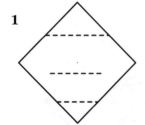

2

3

When the envelopes are folded, distribute index cards, one per person, and pens or pencils. Say: **You have an index card on which to write a very important message, the most important message you can ever deliver to someone! What do you suppose that message might be?** Allow kids to share their thoughts, then say: **The message we want to carry to everyone we know is the message of Jesus' love, forgiveness, and salvation. We want to share the Good News with all people just as Jesus desires us to.**

Invite a volunteer to read aloud Matthew 28:19, 20, then ask:

4

+ *What is so good about the Good News?*
+ *How can the message about Jesus' love and salvation help others?*
+ *In what ways does sharing the message of Jesus' salvation demonstrate our own love for others? for Jesus?*
+ *What are things you could tell others about Jesus?*

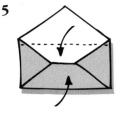

5

Challenge kids to write on their index cards several things they want to share about the message of Jesus' love, forgiveness, and salvation. Then have kids slide the cards into their special-delivery envelopes and seal them with self-adhesive stickers. Tell kids to hand-deliver their messages to someone during the coming week so the Good News about Jesus is shared as He desires.

Love from the Cross

Special love notes and a hidden cross teach Jesus' messages to us.

Ephesians 1:7; 1 Corinthians 1:18

Simple Supplies

✦ brightly colored paper
✦ scissors
✦ pens or pencils
✦ self-adhesive heart stickers
✦ the pattern for the cross on page 55

Before Class

Photocopy the cross pattern from page 55 on brightly colored paper, one pattern page for each person. Fold and prepare one of these cross shapes, then fold over the edges in the swirl pattern and seal the square closed with a self-adhesive heart sticker. Cut the stickers into separate hearts but leave the backing paper in place.

The Fold-n-Hold Message

Hold up your folded square sealed with the heart sticker. Say: **I have a message for all of you. It's a love note from the cross, and it's sent just to you! What messages do you think Jesus wanted to give us from the cross?** Invite kids to tell their ideas and thoughts. Encourage kids to think deeply about why Jesus died for us and what He would tell us about His own messages of love, salvation, hope, and God's power from the cross.

Say: **There are so many messages of love, hope, faith, forgiveness, and salvation that Jesus gave us through His death on the cross—many more messages than we'll probably ever know or realize. But every message the cross gave us is a love note from Jesus! Let's fold some special crosses that will soon contain love notes from the cross to pass along or hold on to as reminders of what the power of love can conquer and complete!**

Distribute the cross patterns and invite someone to read the message in the center square aloud. Discuss the meaning behind Jesus' own words, then say: **Wow! This is one of the strongest messages Jesus gave us from the cross! Jesus wants us to know that when we love and accept Him into our lives and when we believe in His forgiveness and power to save, we will have eternal life even if our bodies stop breathing and living in this world. In other words, Jesus' most powerful message from the cross assures us we can conquer eternal death and live with Him! That's awesome, isn't it? Now follow along as we fold our special cross shapes.**

Demonstrate how to fold each portion of the cross in toward the center to make the spiral card. Be sure everyone completes each step before moving on.

Step 1. Cut out the cross shapes on the solid outlines. (As kids cut out their shapes, remind them how God sent Jesus to teach us about Him. Point out that just as they're following the lines exactly to reach their goal in cutting

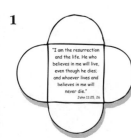

1

"I am the resurrection and the life. He who believes in me will live, even though he dies; and whoever lives and believes in me will never die."
John 11:25, 26

out the crosses, Jesus followed God's desires exactly in bringing us His love, healing, help, and forgiveness.)

Step 2. Fold each portion of the cross in toward the center, creasing each fold well. (As kids fold the edges forward, remind them how Jesus continually bowed to God and His will—even to death on the cross.)

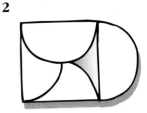

2

Step 3. When the flaps are folded, have kids open them again and write the words to the following verses on the flaps, one verse per flap: *1 Corinthians 1:18, Ephesians 1:7, Romans 5:8,* and *Romans 8:39.* (If kids are very young, have them write the following on the flaps, one word per flap: *Jesus' love forgave us!*)

3

Step 4. When the verses are written on the flaps, hand each person a self-adhesive heart sticker but tell kids not to fasten the notes closed yet.

When the crosses are finished, have kids hold them open and take turns looking up and reading aloud the verses on the ends. Briefly discuss each message and why it's a message of love from the cross. Then ask kids which of these verses, including the verses in the center square, best sum up the most powerful message of love from the cross and why.

Say: **Through His death and resurrection, Jesus gives us powerful messages of hope, forgiveness, God's power, eternal life, and heavenly healing! But most of all, the message from the cross is ... love! Fold your cross into a swirl and place your heart sticker in the center to keep the cross closed. When you get home, invite your family to help open the messages of love from the cross as you read them aloud to one another!**

Fishers of Men

Simple fish remind kids we're all fishers for Jesus.

Luke 5:5-7, 10, 11

Simple Supplies

✦ 8-inch paper squares
✦ markers

Before Class

Make one of these super-simple fish to become famil-iar with the folding directions. (Even the youngest children can easily make these fun fish!) You may wish to use origami paper that is colored on one side and white on the other. This paper is available at most craft stores in precut 8-inch squares.

The Fold-n-Hold Message

Have kids spread out around the room, then begin a quick game of Follow the Leader, tagging each child as you go by and having kids join in the line following you. (Travel in fun ways such as skipping, twirling around, or tiptoeing.) Continue until everyone has joined the line and is following you around the room. Then lead kids in a circle and have them sit in place.

Say: **That was fun! Everyone joined in following the leader everywhere I went! Jesus called His disciples in much the same way. He began by choosing twelve men to follow Him to many places.** Ask:

* ✦ *Who were these twelve men?*
* ✦ *Why do you think Jesus called them to follow Him?*
* ✦ *In what ways is Jesus the best Leader the disciples or even we could ever have?*

Say: **The first disciples Jesus called upon to join Him were fishermen. Their names were Peter and Andrew, and they were brothers who sailed out to cast their nets and fish each day, hoping to catch even a few fish to eat and to sell. Let's do some paper folding as we discover how Jesus called these fishermen to follow Him and who else Jesus invites to join in and follow the Leader!**

Hand out the 8-inch squares of paper and markers. Then demonstrate the easy directions for folding these simple fish. Make sure that kids complete each step before moving on.

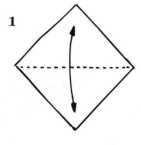

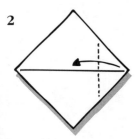

Step 1. Fold an 8-inch square over to make a triangle. Crease the fold, then open the square and spread it flat on the table. (As you fold and unfold the paper, tell kids that fishing nets were folded after fishing, then opened again to dry flat.)

Step 2. Fold the right point over so the tip touches the middle of the square. (As you fold, explain that Jesus and His disciples rowed to the middle of a lake to fish.)

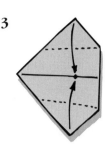

3

Step 3. Flip the paper over. (Tell kids that Jesus told the men to toss their nets overboard and the nets flipped into the water.)

Step 4. Fold the top and bottom points in to meet off-center. (Point out that this shape looks like a boat and that when the nets were pulled in from the sides, they were full of fish—then point out how the shapes also look like fish!) Let kids use markers to add eyes and fishy smiles. (Don't write on the top and bottom fins yet!)

4

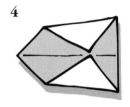

When the fish are folded, say: **Wow! Imagine what the disciples thought when they saw their nets come back filled to overflowing! Though they were surprised by the fish, they had to be more surprised when Jesus told them to follow Him and He would make them fishers of men.** Ask:

- ✦ *What do you think Jesus meant by the phrase "fishers of men"?*
- ✦ *How do we know that Jesus' disciples wanted to choose Jesus as their Leader and become fishers of men?*
- ✦ *In what ways does inviting others to follow Jesus help them? draw us closer to Jesus?*
- ✦ *In what ways can we be fishers of men and invite others to follow Jesus?*

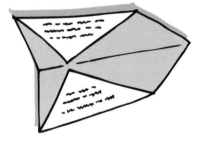

Have kids find Luke 5:10, 11 in their Bibles and invite a volunteer to read the verses aloud. Then have kids write, "From now on you will be fishers of men" on the top fins of their paper fish, and "So they left everything and followed him" on the lower fins. If there's time, play another game of Follow the Leader and have the leader go around and invite kids to follow, one by one, until everyone is following in line.

Friendly Forgiveness

Perky people help kids understand the power of forgiveness.

Luke 6:37; Ephesians 4:32

Simple Supplies

+ 6-inch and 8-inch white paper squares
+ markers
+ ric-rac, sequins, glitter, glue (optional)

Before Class

Use the simple instructions to fold several paper people. Decorate them using markers and craft scraps (if desired). Plan on having kids each fold a large and small paper person. Kids might enjoy turning their paper people into wearable clips or pins. If so, provide craft bar-pins, clip-style clothespins, and tacky craft glue.

The Fold-n-Hold Message

Invite kids to tell what being "forgiving" means and how it helps in our relationships with friends and family members. Encourage kids to tell about times they've forgiven a friend or family member for something that person said or did. Then ask:

+ *In what ways is forgiveness a demonstration of love and compassion?*
+ *Would true compassion and respect be possible without forgiveness? Explain.*
+ *Why do you think God places such a high value on forgiveness?*

Say: **So much of God's Word centers around forgiveness. We learn about what it means to be forgiving of one another and how we all need forgiveness. In fact, we discover through God's Word that our whole eternal life depends on Jesus' forgiveness of our sins! Being forgiving of others is the most wonderful way of expressing our love for others and for God. Without forgiveness in our hearts, we really can't love the way Jesus desires us to love others. Think for a moment about someone you may need to forgive. Maybe it's a family member who said unkind words or teased you in a hurtful way. Or maybe you need to forgive a friend for acting mean or treating you in a selfish way. We'll fold several paper people to represent those people we might need to forgive or to remind us of the importance of offering forgiveness to others as Jesus forgave us.**

Hand a small and large paper square to each person. Then demonstrate the following folding directions for making paper people, referring to the diagrams as needed. Make sure that kids complete each step before moving on.

1

Step 1. Place a square of paper on the table in a diamond shape. Fold opposite sides diagonally so they meet down the center. (You'll have a long diamond shape.) Then fold the bottom triangle upward. Crease the folds well.

Step 2. Fold the bottom edge halfway up the triangle to make a little "boat." Then flip the piece over.

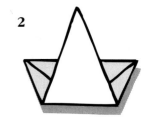

2

Step 3. Fold the two side flaps in to the center to make the "arms." Decorate the folded people as desired. (Do not write under the side arm flaps yet.) If you want a hat or squared-off hair-do, simply fold the top point of the head back and down, creasing well.

When both paper people are folded, invite kids to show their "friends" to one another. (If kids want to make their folded projects into wearable pins or clips, simply glue pin backs or clip-style clothespins to the backs of the paper people.)

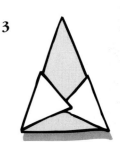

3

Say: **Each paper person looks unique and colorful—just as real people do! But one thing all people have that our paper people don't have is the need to be forgiven and to offer forgiveness. So what does God's Word say about being forgiving? Let's check it out!** Invite volunteers to read aloud Luke 6:37 and Ephesians 4:32. Then ask:

+ *Why is being forgiving so important?*
+ *What will happen if we forgive others?*
+ *What will happen if we don't forgive others? Why?*
+ *Who willingly forgave us of our sins? Why do you think He did this?*
+ *How did Jesus' forgiveness of our sins open the way for us to be closer to God?*
+ *In what ways does our own forgiveness of others open the way for us to be closer to God? to other people?*

Say: **Friends forgive one another, and loving family members forgive one another, too. We can even be forgiving of people we don't know simply because Jesus desires us to be forgiving!** Have kids lift one of the arm flaps on one of their paper people and write, "You forgive me and I forgive you ... " and "Just as Jesus forgives us, too!" under the other flap. Repeat the words for the second paper people. Challenge kids to hand their friendly forgiveness friends to family members or their real friends when they want to offer forgiveness.

FlutterFlies

These fanciful fliers teach about God's attention to details.

Isaiah 14:24

The Fold-n-Hold Message

Act out several animals, birds, fish, or insects for kids to guess, then end your quick guessing game by acting out a butterfly.

When kids have guessed that you're acting out a butterfly say: **God created so many unique living creatures! Just think of all the detail He put into each one: wings for birds to reach nests high in trees, sonar in dolphins to help them swim and navigate the great oceans, even the brown spots on giraffes to help camouflage them. And take butterflies—God designed their delicate wings perfectly so they can soar light as the air. Their beautiful colors help them hide among bright flowers while they safely collect nectar. Butterflies are a perfect example of all the detail, planning, and purpose God put into creation. From fuzzy caterpillars to cocoons and butterflies, God's plans and purpose are detailed, complete, and oh so perfect! Let's fold some fanciful FlutterFlies as we discover more about God's attention to detail and how He has made His purpose and plans complete in the world.**

Distribute the squares of paper, then demonstrate the following step-by-step folding directions using the diagrams. Make sure that kids complete each step before moving on. Allow friends to help if needed.

1

Step 1. Fold a paper square into a triangle. Fold the triangle in half, then open the half back up and place the large triangle on the table.

Step 2. Fold one corner over and past the edge 1 or 2 inches, then unfold that same corner.

2

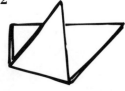

Step 3. Fold the other corner over and past the edge 1 or 2 inches, then unfold that same corner.

Step 4. Pinch the center fold upward to make the FlutterFly's (butterfly) tail. While holding the tail pinched, fold up the side wings on the creases. Decorate the FlutterFlies using watercolor paints or pastel markers, then tape on paper antennas.

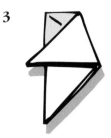

When the FlutterFlies are folded, invite kids to show one another their folded projects and point out any details they might have added. Then say: **I'm so glad that God is a God of details! Because God is wiser than anyone, He knows exactly what details need to go into His plans to accomplish them.**

Read aloud Isaiah 14:24, then ask:

+ *In what ways does God's attention to detail help accomplish His will?*
+ *What are some of the details God included in His creation?*
+ *How does God take care of the details in your life?*
+ *What are some of the details God included in His plan of salvation? Were they accomplished? Explain.*
+ *What would it be like if God didn't care about the small details of our lives?*
+ *How do God's perfect plans and details demonstrate His awesome love for us?*

Invite kids to use markers to write the words to Isaiah 14:24 across the backs of the FlutterFlies. If there's time, let kids fly their folded FlutterFlies around the room.

You're God's Promise!

Pretty swans remind kids that God has a plan for them!

Jeremiah 29:11; Romans 8:28; Philippians 2:13

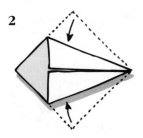

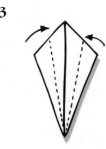

Simple Supplies

✦ 8-inch squares of white or colored paper
✦ fine-tipped markers (optional)

Before Class

Fold a paper swan to become familiar with the directions. Then fold another swan as you practice telling the story of the Ugly Duckling below (folding and holding the swan as indicated in the illustrations). Consider showing pictures of a baby swan and an adult swan so kids can see how a real "ugly duckling" turns into a beautiful bird!

The Fold-n-Hold Message

Hold an 8-inch square of white paper and gather kids in front of you. Say: **I have a story for you about something amazing God planned for a little bird. I'll use this piece of paper to help tell the story.**

Once there was a little, ugly duckling (step 1). **He wasn't anything special and certainly didn't look like he'd amount to much at all. After all, his bill stuck out a little too far** (hold the swan as in step 2), **and his tail feathers were a little too pointed.** (Hold the swan as in step 3.) **No, this was not a pretty little duckling at all! Whenever the little duckling tried to hold his neck up tall and proud** (hold the swan as in step 4), **he would catch a glimpse of himself in the pond** (step 5) **and hang his head.** (Hold the swan as in step 6.) **"What good is a little ugly duckling?" he wondered. But God knew the answer—and God had plans!**

Time passed by, and fall turned to winter, winter to spring, and spring to summer. The little ugly duckling was just stretching from a nap by the pond. He stretched his neck wayyyy up and looked at himself in the water. Oh me, oh my—What did he see? The most beautiful *swan* there could ever be! (Hold the completed swan.) **God saw the promise in that little duckling and knew, through His plans, that duckling would grow to be a beautiful, treasured swan!**

What a beautiful swan the ugly duckling turned out to be! You see, God had a plan for that little bird—and that little bird was like a promise ready to be kept! I really like that story because there have been times when I've felt like an "ugly duckling" wondering where I fit in! Ask:

✦ *Have you ever felt as if you're kind of an ugly duckling? In other words, do you wonder if God has a plan just for you? Explain.*
✦ *In what ways did God's plan and His ultimate control turn the duckling into a beautiful part of God's creation?*

Say: **God had a plan for the duckling, and He has a plan for you, too! You're a promise that God has made, and you can be just what God desires you to be in His plans for you! Let's fold paper swans as we discuss more about being God's promises and how He has a hope and a plan for each of us!**

Hand out the white paper squares, the demonstrate the following step-by-step folding directions. Make sure that kids complete each step before moving on.

Step 1. Fold an 8-inch paper square into a triangle, then open the square again.

Step 2. Diagonally fold two opposite corners of the square along the center fold line. Crease the edges well, then flip the long diamond shape over.

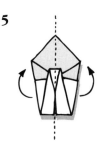

Step 3. Position the diamond so that the long end is pointing downward. Then fold the two upper points over to the center fold line and crease the folds well.

Step 4. Fold the point on the long end of the diamond upward to just below the top point. Crease the fold well. (This is the swan's neck.)

Step 5. Bend the end of the long point downward about an inch to make the swan's "head." Then fold the swan in half and backward along the center fold line.

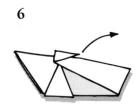

Step 6. Hold the swan and lift the neck and head upward so the swan "looks at you." Slightly spread the body so the swan sits upright. If you want, use a fine-tipped marker to add eyes and other features.

When the swans are finished, say: **Just as you completed each step in taking a plain piece of paper and turning it into a beautiful swan, we complete steps God sets before us on our way to being all He has planned for us to be.** Ask:

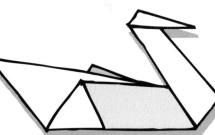

> ✦ *Why do you think it takes time to become all that God desires us to be?*
> ✦ *Who is in control of our futures and the plans set out for us? Explain.*
> ✦ *In what ways are we promises from God?*
> ✦ *How does God help us turn from being toddlers into people of faith who serve God in beautiful ways?*
> ✦ *Could God ever create truly "ugly ducklings"? Explain.*

Read aloud Jeremiah 29:11; Romans 8:28; and Philippians 2:13. Then say: **God has a plan and a purpose set out for each of us. And though accomplishing God's will in our lives takes time, just as it took time for the duckling to become all God had designed for him, God's plans will be done! It often feels as if we're ugly ducklings with no part in God's plans, but that's not true. Each of us is like a promise God has created, and He will help us accomplish those promises through His plans and purpose. When we follow God, choose to obey Him, and seek to learn what God's will for us might be, we turn into all God desires us to be! Keep your swan as a reminder that God's not done with you yet—He's only beginning to help you become a beautiful swan in His kingdom!**

Dove of Love

These folded dove mobiles remind us to obey God.

Matthew 3:16, 17; Luke 11:28

The Fold-n-Hold Message

Invite kids to tell about rules they have at school or at home that must be obeyed. Encourage kids to explain why these rules are important to obey and what happens if they disobey rules made by teachers or parents.

After everyone who wants to has shared, say: **There are rules for living everywhere we go. Whether it's traffic laws to rules on playgrounds and at home, obeying rules allows us to live in safety, peace, and happiness. Rules are made by people who love us and care about our welfare—and we want to obey the rules and those people who love and care for us. Obedience to parents, teachers, rules, and especially God is very important indeed! Even Jesus obeyed when it came to doing as God, His Father, desired Him to do.** Invite a volunteer to read aloud Matthew 3:16, 17. Then ask:

+ *In what ways did Jesus obey God?*
+ *Why do you think Jesus chose to be obedient to His heavenly Father?*
+ *How do we know that Jesus' obedience pleased God?*

Say: **When God's Spirit, looking like a dove, descended to rest above Jesus, He knew His Father was pleased with Him. Jesus chose to obey God because He loved and respected God and because Jesus knew that God is all-powerful, with all authority in heaven and on earth!**

Let's fold a dove that reminds us of the importance of being obedient to God, just as Jesus was obedient. Then we'll discover more about what God's Word teaches us concerning obedience.

Distribute the pattern pages and scissors. Demonstrate the following step-by-step folding directions, referring to the diagrams as needed. Make sure that kids complete each step before moving on.

1

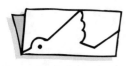

Step 1. Fold the pattern page in half, creasing it well. Cut along the solid outlines of the dove. Then cut out the three verse cards.

Step 2. Slightly unfold the dove's wings, then tape or glue the two sides of the dove's head, body, and tail wings. Do not glue the two large wings together!

2

Step 3. Fold the dove's wings outward.

3

Step 4. Cut a hanging loop from thread or fishing line and tape it between the folded wings. Then suspend the verse cards from the lower edges of the dove using thread or fishing line.

4

When the Dove of Love mobiles are folded and finished, say: **Think back to the step-by-step directions for making the doves. What might have happened if you hadn't obeyed the folding directions?** Allow kids to share their ideas, then continue: **When we don't obey, things don't work right! If it's important to obey paper folding directions for projects to turn out right, imagine how much more important it is to obey God!** Read aloud Luke 11:28, then ask:

✦ *What does God's Word say will happen if we obey God?*
✦ *What are ways we can obey God each day?*

Say: **One of the best ways to obey God is to learn His Word and then put it to use in our lives. Hang your Dove of Love mobile at home in a place where you and your family can be reminded of how Jesus obeyed God and how we're to obey God, too. And help each other obey God by learning the verses on the verse cards!**

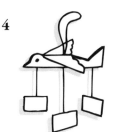

A Treasure to Measure

Nifty boxes and treasures remind kids of the value of Scripture.

Psalm 119:11, 105

Simple Supplies

♦ scissors, markers, glue
♦ self-adhesive hook-and-loop fasteners
♦ copies of the treasure box from page 57
♦ copies of the Scripture cards from page 58

Before Class

Photocopy and enlarge the treasure-box pattern and the Scripture cards onto bright card stock, one box enlarged to 125 percent and one set of cards per child plus a few extras. Assemble a treasure box and place a set of Scripture cards in the box. For more glitzy fun, provide glitter and sequins to embellish the boxes!

The Fold-n-Hold Message

Gather kids and ask them to name a great treasure that they wish they could have. Suggestions might include a fancy new bike or computer, a trip around the world, or even huge mansions for their families to live in. Then ask kids where people sometimes keep great treasures. Answers might include a bank vault, a hidden treasure cave, or a locked box.

Say: **People always seem to dream of having or owning great treasures such as fancy jewelry kept in locked chests, garages full of fancy cars, or vaults filled with money or gold. And though most people dream of treasures, few actually find such great wealth. But I know of a treasure even more precious than gems and gold, a treasure that will last forever and never tarnish or fade away.**

Let's fold fancy treasure chests to remind us of the greatest treasure we have and can make our own. After we fold our treasure boxes, we'll discover just what this treasure without measure is

Distribute the treasure-box patterns and scissors (but not the Scripture cards yet). Demonstrate the following step-by-step folding directions using the diagrams to assemble the boxes. Make sure that kids complete each step before moving on. Allow friends to help if needed.

1

Step 1. Cut out the treasure box along the dark, solid lines.

2

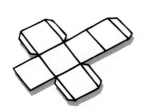

Step 2. Fold both of the side flaps upward. Now fold all four tabs inward. Place a bit of glue along each tab.

Step 3. Fold the front and back flaps upward and press them against the glue on the tabs to form a box.

Step 4. Fold the top of the box and the tab forward along the dotted lines to make the lid. Decorate the treasure box, then fasten a bit of self-adhesive hook-and-loop fastener to the underside of the lid tab and to the top of the box underneath the tab to keep the box closed.

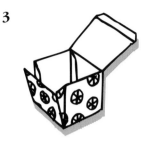

3

When the treasure boxes are finished and embellished, invite kids to tell what kind of treasure could fit into these boxes and last forever. Then say: **There aren't enough earthly riches to fit inside of this box, and besides, treasures of the world eventually fade away or become lost. But the treasure we have in God's Word lasts forever! God's Word is the greatest treasure we can have and own today. And do you know the best part? When we use this amazing treasure, it only becomes greater!**

Hand out the Scripture pages and let kids cut apart the verse cards and line them up on the floor or table in order of the verse numbers (all the verses are from Psalm 119). Invite kids to form pairs or trios and quickly read the verses with their partners. Then say: **There is so much this great treasure does for us when we learn, understand, and use God's Word!** Ask:

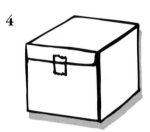

4

- *How does God's Word help us?*
- *In what ways does God's Word save us and keep us from harm?*
- *How can putting God's Word to use in our lives bring us closer to God and others?*
- *In what ways does God's Word give us comfort for today and hope for the future?*
- *How does learning God's Word keep us from disobeying God?*
- *In what ways is God's Word a great treasure that lasts forever?*

Say: **When we take the time and make the effort to really learn and understand God's Word, we can begin to use the power of the Word in our lives. Some people think they can't learn or memorize God's Word, but would God give us His Word and want us to learn it if it was not possible? Of course not!** Read aloud Psalm 119:73, then continue: **God will help you learn, understand, and use His precious Word. And it pleases God when we take the time to really learn what He says. God honors us when we learn and use His Word.**

Have kids place the Scripture cards in their treasure boxes. Then challenge kids to work on learning, understanding, and using one verse each week for the next eight weeks.

Witness Triangles

3-D tracts help kids share the kingdom with others!

Romans 3:23; 1 Timothy 1:15

The Fold-n-Hold Message

Invite kids to tell about times they tried to tell a friend, family member, or someone else about Jesus. Encourage kids to tell what they shared about Jesus and what the reaction from that person was.

After several kids have responded, say: **When you have really good news or know about something wonderful that can help others, you naturally want to share that news! Telling others about Jesus is no different. When we share about Jesus and tell others what Jesus has done in our own lives, it's called "witnessing." Witnessing takes the Good News about Jesus and makes it even more personal because we share some of the wonderful things Jesus has done for us and how Jesus helps in our lives and gives us hope.** Ask:

+ *Why is telling others about Jesus so important?*
+ *How can it help others if we witness to them about all that Jesus has done in our own lives?*
+ *Why do you think Jesus desires us to tell others about Him and to share what He means to us?*

Say: **Jesus wants us to be powerful witnesses for Him and to share the Good News about what Jesus has done for us. But it's sometimes hard to know where to begin sharing. Let's fold some cool 3-D triangles that have good suggestions for where to begin talking to others about Jesus. Then we'll discover more about what it means to witness to others.**

Hand out the pattern pages and scissors. Demonstrate the following step-by-step folding directions for assembling the triangles. Make sure that kids complete each step before moving on. Allow friends to help if needed.

1

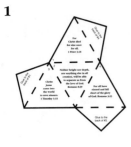

Step 1. Cut out the shape on the solid lines. Fold back on the dotted lines.

Step 2. Form a triangle shape and tape or glue as directed on the pattern.

2

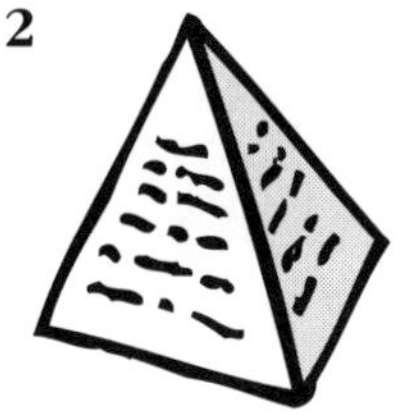

When the 3-D triangles are folded and assembled, invite kids to take turns reading the verses on the sides aloud. Then say: **Wow! What powerful verses we've just read! These verses sum up the who, what, and why in telling others about Jesus. Let's see if you can identify them! I'll ask a question, and you can answer by reading the appropriate verse.** Ask:

+ *Why did Jesus come into the world?*
+ *Who has sinned and is in need of forgiveness?*
+ *Who is the only one who can forgive our sins and who died for our sins?*
+ *Can anything separate us, once we've been forgiven, from God? Explain.*

Say: **Each one of these verses is a great place to begin to tell others about Jesus and what He's done for us—and for you personally. You can ask others if they know that we're all in need of forgiveness. Or you can ask if they knows Jesus died just for them so they could live with God forever. What are other ways you can use these verses to begin talking with others about Jesus?**

Allow kids to share their thoughts, then say: **When a personal witness is written down and the Good News shared, it's often called a "tract." Tracts can be helpful so people can read more about Jesus when they're ready. Think about someone you could give your triangle-shaped tract to. Then strike up a conversation about Jesus and all He's done for you and present that person with your nifty triangle tract!**

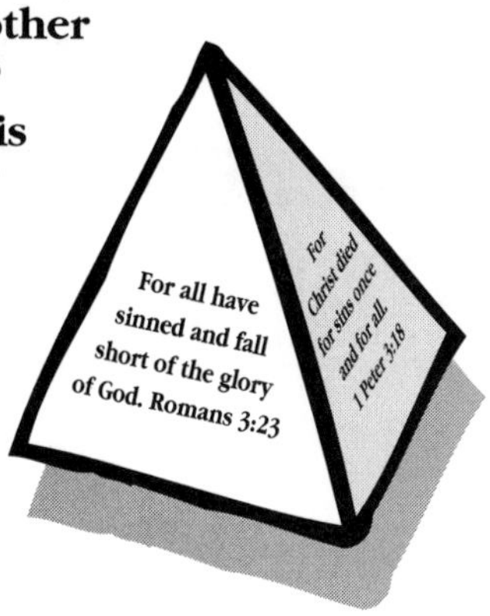

For all have sinned and fall short of the glory of God. Romans 3:23

For Christ died for sins once and for all. 1 Peter 3:18

Super-Star Promises

Nifty stars remind kids that God's promises to them are always kept.

Joshua 23:14; Romans 4:20, 21

Simple Supplies

- ✦ stiff paper
- ✦ scissors, tape
- ✦ curling ribbon
- ✦ glitter glue
- ✦ index cards
- ✦ fine-tipped markers
- ✦ copies of the star pattern from page 60

Before Class

Photocopy the star pattern on stiff white or bright yellow card-stock paper. Copy at least three star patterns for each person plus three for yourself. Prepare and fold three stars and outline them with glitter glue. Tape strings to the tops of the stars, then tie curled ribbon to the string. Later in the lesson you'll add a verse card to your star "bouquet."

The Fold-n-Hold Message

Invite kids to tell about the toughest promise they ever made and kept. Encourage kids to tell why the promise was so hard to keep and what might have happened had the promise not been kept. Then say: **Promises can be so easy to make—and so tough to keep at times! Promises such as cleaning our rooms or being on time for school may not be too hard to keep. But bigger promises such as never saying a mean word again or promising to solve someone's problems may be too tough to keep in the way we want to keep them. And we all know there's nothing so sad or disappointing as a broken promise, because once a promise is broken, it can never be put together again in perfect condition. We try but can't always keep every promise we make, but there's someone who can!** Ask:

- ✦ *Why do you think God always keeps His promises?*
- ✦ *How does knowing that God keeps His promises give us hope and strengthen our faith in Him?*
- ✦ *In what ways is keeping His promises a demonstration of God's love for us?*

Say: **God has the authority to make any promise, and He has the power to keep every one He makes! Remember how God promised Abraham one starry night that he would become the father of many nations even though Abraham had no children?** Invite kids to retell the story of God's promise to Abraham (from Genesis 15:5 and 17:19). Explain that the word *covenant* means "promise" and that God promised Abraham and his wife Sarah, even though they were very old, a child who would grow into a mighty nation. Point out that God promised as many children as there are stars in the sky!

Say: **Imagine what Abraham thought as he gazed at all the stars in the heavens. He must have been amazed thinking that his descendants would number** so many! I'm sure Abraham thought this was the biggest promise God had ever made—yet God kept his promise to Abraham, just as God keeps every promise He makes to us. Let's fold glittery stars to remind us that God has the power and love to keep every promise He makes. Then we'll discover what God promises us.

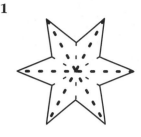

Hand each person three star patterns. Demonstrate the following step-by-step folding directions using the diagrams. Make sure that kids complete each step before moving on. Allow friends to help if needed.

Step 1. Cut out the star on the solid outline.

Step 2. Pinch upward on the longer dotted lines and downward on the smaller dotted lines to create an up-and-down look for the star. (This will give the star a 3-D look.).

When each person has made several stars, outline the stars using glitter glue. Tape varying lengths of string to the tops of the stars, then knot the ends of the strings together. Finally, tie curling ribbon around the knot and let several strands hang down.

When the string and ribbons are in place, say: **Your super stars are beautiful! And they all represent promises God has made and kept to us. But what are some of the promises God makes to us?** Encourage kids to name some of God's promises, such as His promise never to flood the world again (from Noah and the ark), His promise to love us, to answer us, to help us, to guide us, to give us a hope and a future. Make sure to mention God's greatest promise: salvation through Jesus, which He has kept! Read aloud Joshua 23:14 and Romans 4:20, 21. Then ask:

✦ *In what ways do God's promises give us strength for today? hope for tomorrow?*
✦ *What promise of God's gives you the most comfort? Why?*
✦ *How can we thank God for His promises and for His love and power to honor each one?*

Distribute the index cards and pens or fine-tipped markers. Invite kids to write Joshua 23:14 on their cards ("You know with all your heart and soul that not one of all the good promises the LORD your God gave you has failed. Every promise has been fulfilled; not one has failed.") Then have kids tape the verse card to the curling ribbon at the top of the stars.

Lead kids in reading the verse aloud, then say: **Read this verse each day for the next week as you think about all of the promises God has made to you and how He has kept or is keeping each one. What a starry-eyed, heart-filled demonstration of His love!**

A Cup of Kindness

Nifty folded cups teach kids about offering kindness to all.

Mark 9:41; Ephesians 4:32

Simple Supplies

+ 8-inch paper squares (two per person)
+ markers
+ a pitcher of cold water

Before Class

Fold one of these cups to become familiar with the simple directions. Plan on letting kids fold at least two cups (or one for each member of the family plus one extra). You'll be using these cool cups to serve each other a drink of water during class.

The Fold-n-Hold Message

Gather kids and ask them how we can tell a Christian from someone who might not know Jesus personally or follow Him. Ask:

+ *Can you pick out people who love Jesus by the color of their hair or how tall or old they are? Explain.*
+ *What lets others become aware that we know, love, and follow Jesus?*
+ *How do our actions and the kindnesses we show others clue them into our love for Jesus?*
+ *In what ways do our attitudes and love influence our actions and the kindness we offer to others?*
+ *What are attitudes Jesus would want us to have in our lives that would help us offer kindness to others?*

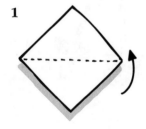

Say: **As Christians, we're very much known by our actions. It's easy to say "I'm a Christian," but if our actions don't match those words, people see right through us—and so does God! As Christians, we want to offer a cup of kindness, love, and compassion to everyone we meet. As we fold cool cups that we can really drink from, we'll discover more about what it means to offer a cup of kindness to others.**

Hand out the paper squares, then demonstrate the following step-by-step folding directions for making these simple drinking cups. Make sure that kids complete each step before moving on. Encourage kids to offer a "cup of kind help" to one another if needed.

Step 1. Fold the paper square in half diagonally.

Step 2. Crease the fold you just made well so the triangle lies flat on the table.

Step 3. Fold the lower corners of the triangle so the tips touch the middles of the opposite sides.

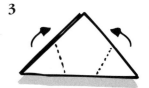

Step 4. Fold the top triangular flaps down to rest on each side of the paper cup. Gently poke your fingers into the cup to spread it out a bit. (Have kids fold a second paper cup before moving on.)

When everyone has folded two paper cups, say: **You did such a fine job folding these cups. Did you know we can really drink from them? In a moment we'll share cold drinks of water from these special cups, but first there's a verse I want to share with you!** Invite a volunteer to read aloud Mark 9:41, then ask:

✦ *What does this verse teach us about how others will know we love Jesus?*
✦ *In what ways does offering someone who's thirsty a cup of water show we care about Jesus?*
✦ *What other ways are we to offer kindness to others in Jesus' name?*
✦ *If we offer the cup of kindness to others in Jesus' name, what will happen?*

Say: **Jesus spent His entire life offering the cup of kindness to others—and to us—over and over again. And Jesus wants us to do the same, for when we're kind and compassionate to others, we're showing love to and for Jesus! That's a pretty important cup we can serve one another, isn't it? Let's take a moment right now to serve one another a cool drink. Choose one of your cups to fill and offer to someone.** Make sure everyone is offered a cup of water and encourage kids to sip their drinks quickly so the water won't soak through the paper cups.

When everyone has served and also been offered a drink of water, read aloud Ephesians 4:32, then briefly discuss other ways to show kindness to one another. If you would like, have kids write the words to Ephesians 4:32 on one of their cups. End with a prayer thanking Jesus for His own kind love and asking for His help in always offering a cup of kindness to people we meet.

Love Knots

Clever paper knots remind kids that we're joined forever with Jesus.

Romans 8:35, 38, 39

Simple Supplies

◆ a roll of gift wrap
◆ scissors
◆ fine-tipped permanent markers

Before Class

Cut festive or shiny gift wrap into 20-by-4-inch lengths, one per person plus several extras. Practice folding and "tying" a paper knot to show kids and to become familiar with the directions. Kids will each make a paper knot, then add a verse to the ends of the knots.

The Fold-n-Hold Message

Challenge kids to think of ways they may be joined to others. Suggestions might include being joined with our families, being bonded with good friends, and even being joined to the human race forever. Encourage kids to tell how it feels knowing we're joined with others in different ways, then ask:

◆ *What bonds or ties hold us together with others?*
◆ *What role does love play in how we're joined to others?*
◆ *In what way does being joined with others give us a sense of identity, belonging, acceptance, and even hope?*

Say: **Sometimes people move in and out of our lives, such as classmates at school, friends we meet at camp or in our neighborhoods, and even people we see often at the grocery store. Not everyone we meet is going to be a part of our lives forever. But family members will be there for us as well as good friends. And there is someone who we'll always be joined to forever. Who do you suppose that is?**

Lead kids to understand that Jesus has promised to be with us always and that we'll be joined together in love with Him forever. Then continue: **Once we accept Jesus as our personal friend and savior, we have His assurance that He will always be with us; that we'll be joined together with Him in love for all time. Our bond with Jesus is like a love knot binding us close forever! Isn't that an awesome truth? Let's fold cool paper love knots to symbolize being joined with Jesus in love forever. Then we'll discover more about what it means to be with Jesus for eternity.**

Distribute the long paper strips. Demonstrate the following step-by-step folding directions using the diagrams. Make sure that kids complete each step before moving on. Encourage friends to help one another if needed.

1

Step 1. Fold the long strip of wrapping paper in half lengthwise.

Step 2. Fold the strip of paper in a V-shape.

Step 3. Fold the left side of the strip diagonally downward and overlapping the right side of the paper strip.

Step 4. Repeat this step for the left side, then slide the end through the hole. Pull gently on the ends, then gently flatten the love knot by pressing down on it (as it lays on a table).

When the love knots are folded, hand each person a fine-tipped permanent marker. Invite kids to get into small groups of three or four and brainstorm reasons we're tied with love to Jesus. Suggestions might include that we're bonded through love, forgiveness, faith, truth, Jesus' salvation, hope, and Christ's blood on the cross. Then have kids write those ways on one side of their paper love knots.

When kids are finished writing, invite them to share what they've written. Then read aloud Romans 8:35, 38, 39 and ask:

+ ***Once we're joined or tied to Jesus, can anything break that bond of love? Explain.***
+ ***Why do you think Jesus wants us to be tied in love to Him?***
+ ***In what ways does it give us hope to know we never have to face tomorrow without Jesus?***

Have kids flip their love knots over and write Romans 8:39 across the paper. Then challenge kids to learn this verse over the next week or two. Review the verse often in class to help kids lock away the learning!

Flip-Flops

Nifty fold 'n flip reminders of changing our attitudes for Jesus.

1 Corinthians 2:16; Philippians 4:7

Simple Supplies

+ white or colored copy paper
+ pens or markers
+ copies of the Flip-Flop handout from page 61

Before Class

Photocopy page 61 for each person plus a few extras. Leave the page intact and practice the folding directions for making the upright character flip-flop so it's upside down and then back to upright again. Kids will love this cool talk and slick paper-folding trick!

The Fold-n-Hold Message

Invite kids to tell what kinds of attitudes we have before knowing or loving Jesus. Suggestions might include attitudes of selfishness, unkindness, impatience, anger, and hopelessness. Then ask kids how our attitudes change when we discover Jesus' love and accept His forgiveness in our lives. Encourage kids to tell how it feels to have changes of heart and attitudes, then ask:

+ ***In what ways are our actions and words tied to our attitudes and the conditions of our hearts?***
+ ***What kinds of actions might accompany attitudes that are not in line with what Jesus desires? In other words, how do we act before knowing or following Jesus?***
+ ***Why is it necessary to change our attitudes and the conditions of our hearts when we choose to love and follow Jesus?***

Say: **When we live without Jesus as our focus and without the Holy Spirit to teach and lead us, our attitudes may be self-centered and too much focused on the world and its temptations. When we choose to open our lives to Jesus, our attitudes must do a flip-flop and change for Jesus! Let's fold paper as we discover more about what I mean.**

Distribute the handouts, then demonstrate the following step-by-step folding directions to make the characters on the handouts flip-flop, then flip-flop back again. Be sure to use the accompanying statements with each step!

1

Step 1. Begin with the figure "standing upright" on the page and facing your audience. Then fold the photocopied page in half, top to bottom so the figure is on the inside of the fold and you've made a long rectangle. As you fold the paper, say: **Before we know Jesus, we think everything is**

fine—even if we're being selfish, unkind, or stubborn. But those attitudes make us fold over when we see how ugly we truly feel inside!

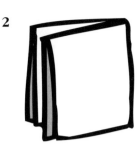

Step 2. Fold the rectangle in half side-to-side from right to left as you say: **We may turn one direction and become even more frustrated and angry. Our attitudes may become even worse!**

Step 3. Turn the paper around, then unfold it to show the rectangle shape. Say: **Our negative attitudes and self-centered behaviors can really turn us about and confuse us.**

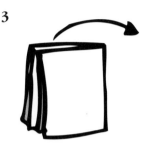

Step 4. Open up the rectangle, and the figure will be upside down! Say: **Our attitudes become so wrong and negative that we're turned completely opposite from the way Jesus desires us to be! We need a real change of heart!**

Step 5. Repeat the steps to make the figure upright again. As you refold and turn the paper, say: **We need to flip-flop our attitudes. And when we turn to face and follow Jesus, something wonderful happens! We become giving and sharing, serving and caring—and find ourselves back on our feet with new hearts and attitudes for Jesus!**

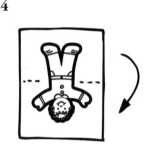

When the characters on the patterns have been folded and flip-flopped until they've returned to their standing positions, say: **Wow! I guess the Bible is right when it says we become new creations in Jesus when we accept and follow Him!** Ask:

+ *Why do attitudes become so selfish when we don't know Jesus?*
+ *How does Jesus help turn us around and give us new attitudes?*
+ *What kinds of changes are there in our actions and words when we know, love, and follow Jesus?*
+ *Which is more productive and draws us closer to others and God: selfish attitudes or selfless attitudes? Why?*
+ *How can we work at flip-flopping selfish behaviors and mean words into new, kind attitudes for Jesus?*

Read aloud 1 Corinthians 2:16 and Philippians 4:7, then say: **When we love Jesus we naturally want to become more like Him. We choose to be cheerful, helpful, patient, kind, compassionate, and thankful. Our hearts feel new and fresh, and our attitudes become changed and alive in Christ! Present this object talk to your friends and family members to remind them of how we must flip-flop our selfish hearts in exchange for the new, loving attitudes that Jesus desires us to have.** Fold the figures upside down, then right-side up once more. If there's time, have kids color their Flip-Flop figures.

A Cheerful Choice!

Cute puppets remind kids that being happy is a choice we make.

Proverbs 15:13, 15; 17:22

Simple Supplies

+ 6-inch squares of copy paper
+ colorful markers

Before Class

Practice folding this simple but fun puppet. Use white copy paper or colored paper. Add features and lips so your puppet pal can happily "chat" about how great it is to choose being happy! (For even more fun, provide scraps of ribbon, fake hair, glitter, and more to embellish puppets. Don't forget the glue!)

The Fold-n-Hold Message

Invite kids to begin the object talk by making some choices. Read the situations below, then have kids give a thumbs-up sign if they could be happy in response to that situation. Let kids give a thumbs-down sign if they would not be happy.

+ *Your best shirt got a big grass stain on it.*
+ *Your birthday cake was a different flavor from what you'd hoped.*
+ *The sun was shining for your ballgame.*
+ *Your best friend couldn't come over to play.*
+ *Your mom made your favorite meal for dinner.*
+ *Your mom made her favorite meal for dinner.*
+ *You missed a day of school because of a cold.*

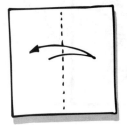

After kids signal their responses, say: **Wow! Your choices really were different from one another! There are lots of things that make some people cheerful while others aren't happy about those same things or situations. It's easy to feel happy when something makes us feel good, like having our favorite meal or receiving birthday gifts. It's not always easy to remain cheerful and positive when we're faced with something unpleasant. It's important to realize that happiness is a choice we make—every day, in each situation we face. Let's fold slick little finger puppets to explore how choosing to be cheerful is one of the best choices we can make!**

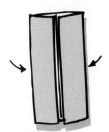

Hand out the 6-inch paper squares. Demonstrate the following step-by-step folding directions using the diagrams. Make sure that kids complete each step before moving on. Invite friends to cheerfully help one another if needed.

Step 1. Fold a 6-inch square in half lengthwise, then open the paper again.

Step 2. Fold both sides in to meet in the center, then fold the paper in half again lengthwise.

Step 3. Fold the bottom layer up to meet the top.

3

Step 4. Fold the back layer (at the top) backward to the bottom.

Step 5. Insert your index finger and thumb in the pockets at the top and bottom of the folded shape. When you open and close your fingers, the puppet's "mouth" will open and close as if it's talking! Use markers to draw a cheerful face and smiling lips on the puppet. (Kids can even color in hair, hair bows, eyeglasses, or freckles!)

When the perky puppets are folded, say: **What cheerful-looking puppets I see! I think they're cheerful because they know being happy makes us feel better. Did you know that it takes many more facial muscles to frown than it does to smile? That's because God wanted us to have cheerful faces, hearts, and spirits! Let's explore what God's Word says about being cheerful and what good things happen when we choose to be happy.** Invite volunteers to read aloud Proverbs 15:13, 15; and 17:22, then ask:

4

- ✦ *What good things come about when we're cheerful rather than angry, disappointed, or frustrated?*
- ✦ *What does choosing to be cheerful in every situation reveal about our trust in God?*
- ✦ *Does it help matters when we choose to be angry, frustrated, or impatient? Explain.*
- ✦ *How can choosing to be cheerful help things look brighter and more hopeful?*
- ✦ *In what ways does trusting and loving God help us be more cheerful and happy in every situation—even in the most trying of times?*

5

Say: **Having worries, troubles, frustrations, and sad feelings is a natural part of being human. But it's how we choose to respond to those feelings and situations that makes all the difference! And when we choose to be cheerful and put our faith in God and His power to help us, being happy isn't such a hard choice to make!** Have kids use markers to write Proverbs 15:13 inside the smiling mouths of their finger puppets. If there's time, let the "puppets" tell things to be happy about.

Best Blessing

Awesome oysters with pearls remind kids of their heavenly treasures.

Matthew 13:45, 46

Simple Supplies

- ✦ paper plates
- ✦ tacky craft glue
- ✦ sheets of pink tissue paper
- ✦ construction paper (pink and white)
- ✦ scissors, markers
- ✦ large faux pearls or ping-pong balls

Before Class

Follow the directions for making one of these adorable oysters that hold "pearls." Make sure you have one faux pearl or ping-pong ball for each person. Most craft stores will have large plastic pearls, or you can use ping-pong balls for pearls if you desire.

The Fold-n-Hold Message

Ask kids to tell what their greatest treasures or possessions are. Suggestions might include favorite toys, savings bonds, piggy banks, computers, or even pets or family members. Encourage kids to explain why the things they've named are considered so valuable to them. Then share something you consider very valuable and why you treasure it. Say: **We all have things, people, and treasures that we hold near and dear and regard as very valuable. When something is very close to our hearts, we treasure it. Think about your faith, God, His Word, and Jesus for a moment and consider all of the things you treasure about them.** Ask:

1

- ✦ *What treasures do we have in God and Jesus?*
- ✦ *Why do you consider these to be treasures?*
- ✦ *How much do you think these treasures are worth? Can any price be put on them? Explain.*
- ✦ *How much would you be willing to give to keep these invaluable treasures? Why?*

Say: **We have so many riches and treasures in God, His Word, and in Jesus our Savior! And they're the most valuable treasures we will ever know! Our treasures in God and Christ are like a big, beautiful, invaluable pearl that shines into our lives with treasures more deep than we can comprehend. Let's fold paper oysters with pearls to remind us of the immense treasures we have in God's kingdom.**

2

Hand each person a paper plate and a "pearl." Demonstrate the following step-by-step directions for folding and assembling the paper oysters and pearls. Make sure that kids complete each step before moving on.

Step 1. Fold a paper plate in half so the curved rim edges touch.

Step 2. Crumple a half-sheet of pink tissue paper and glue it on the inside bottom surface of the paper "oyster."

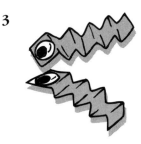

Step 3. Accordion-fold (back and forth) two 1-by-3-inch strips of pink (or white) construction paper. Glue the ends of the accordion-folded strips to the pink tissue paper, then glue paper eyes on the other ends of the strips.

Step 4. Glue a large plastic pearl or ping-pong ball in the center of the pink tissue paper.

When the paper oysters with pearls are folded and finished, say: **Your oysters are so cute! Oysters make beautiful pearls in the ocean, and the pearls are greatly valued. But only God makes the priceless treasures we have in Him! And we want to do everything and give everything to have this heavenly treasure. Listen to a short story about a man who sold everything to buy a perfect pearl.** Invite volunteers to read aloud Matthew 13:45, 46. Then ask:

✦ *In what ways does the pearl in this story represent the treasure we have in God's kingdom?*
✦ *Was the man wise or foolish for giving everything to have the pearl? Explain.*
✦ *Are we wise or foolish for wanting to give God our all so we can seek His kingdom? Explain.*
✦ *What are you willing to give up to hold on to the treasure you have in God and Jesus? Why are you willing?*

Say: **The kingdom of heaven, God, His Word, and Jesus are more precious than we can ever know. And even though they're the most valuable treasures we have, there's no way a price can be put on them. When we desire the richness of God and Christ, we're willing to give up whatever we can to have them. But do you know the best part? They're free by God's great grace! When we choose to know, love, and follow God and His Son Jesus, this immense treasure is freely given to us. And I am so very thankful, aren't you? Each time you see your pearl, give God thanks for one of the treasures He's given you!** End by having kids write the words to Luke 12:34 on the top "shells" of the oysters.

Popping Up with Thanks

Perky pop-up cards remind kids to express their thanks.

Psalm 7:17; 1 Timothy 2:1

Simple Supplies

+ white card stock or construction paper
+ colored markers
+ scissors
+ copies of the card pattern from page 62

Before Class

Photocopy the card pattern from page 62 on stiff, white paper, one copy for each person plus several extras. Cut out and fold one of the cards, then decorate it according to the directions. For even more crafty fun, provide craft scraps such as sequins, glitter, bits of ribbon, and glue for kids to use in embellishing these special thank-you cards.

The Fold-n-Hold Message

Ask kids to tell about times they received some much-needed help or encouragement from someone. Encourage kids to share why they needed help or encouragement and how that special someone provided for their needs.

After everyone who wants to has had a chance to share, say: **Everyone needs help, encouragement, or support now and then. It feels pretty frustrating or hopeless when we're in need, doesn't it? And just think of how great it feels when someone special offers to help us!** Ask:

+ *How is compassion and love shown when someone helps us?*
+ *How should we respond to people when they offer us help or encouragement?*
+ *Why is expressing our thanks so important?*
+ *Does thanks need to be expressed, or is it enough just to be silently glad that we received help? Explain.*

Say: **Thanks can certainly be a silent, wonderful feeling in the heart, but it also needs to have a voice! We need to express our thanks when someone takes the time and effort to be there for us—and especially when God offers us His loving help! Having a spirit of thankfulness allows our love to flow over to God and others in wonderful ways! Think of someone you want to thank for something he or she has done for you. Now let's fold fun pop-up cards to express thanks to those special people.**

Hand out the card patterns and scissors. Demonstrate the following simple folding directions to prepare the pop-up cards. Make sure that kids complete each step before moving on.

Step 1. Cut out the card on the solid outline.

1

"I will give thanks to the Lord because of his righteousness and will sing praise to the name of the Lord Most High."

Psalm 7:17

2

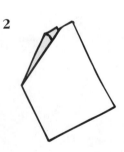

Step 2. Fold the scalloped pop-up portion of the card down and inward on the dotted lines so the pop-up section lies flat inside the card when it's closed.

Step 3. Open the card again. Draw a design in the pop-up portion of the card, such as a bright bouquet, clouds and sunshine, or even fluffy popcorn with smiley faces! Color in the design, then fold the card closed. On the front of the card, write "Popping Up with Thanks for You!"

Popping Up with Thanks for You!

When the pop-up cards are folded and finished, invite a volunteer to read the verse on the inside of the card. Then say: **Wow! What a beautiful thank-you to God! When we want to express our thanks, we always begin by thanking and praising God because it's through God that all help flows to us. God sends others our way to help or encourage us in amazing ways. When we want to express the thanks in our hearts, we begin by thanking God.** Ask:

+ *Why is it good to give thanks to God?*
+ *How does thanking God also express our love to Him?*
+ *What are ways we can thank God each day for His blessings and help?*

Read aloud 1 Timothy 2:1, then say: **After expressing our thanks to God, we express our thanks to others who have helped us or given us support and encouragement. Let's express our thanks right now. Write a short note of thanks to the person you wish to thank with your special thank-you card.** Allow a few minutes for kids to write their notes, then end your time together by having kids take turns reading their thank-you notes.

"I will give thanks to the Lord because of his righteousness and will sing praise to the name of the Lord Most High."

Psalm 7:17

Thank you for helping me with my spelling homework. You're the best.

Eagle's Wings

Soaring paper eagles teach kids that God gives us hope to soar on!

Isaiah 40:31

Simple Supplies

- ✦ 12-inch black paper squares
- ✦ white gel pens

Before Class

Practice folding and flying a paper eagle so you become familiar with the directions. Add eyes and the verse using a white gel pen so the markings show on the black paper. If you'd like a bald eagle, simply color the head with the white gel pen, then add eyes using a black pen or marker.

The Fold-n-Hold Message

Begin by telling kids you have a riddle for them about a creature God has made that they all know. Read the following riddle and encourage kids to guess which animal you're describing.

I may be bald, and my cry is loud;
I'm a creature of God's—powerful and proud.
Supported on the wind as it whooshes by,
I climb and rise high in the sky!
Who am I?

After kids guess that you're describing an eagle, say: **Aren't eagles beautiful? Close your eyes. Now just imagine how wonderful it feels to soar on the wind as it lifts you up. Feel how light you are and how clearly you can see—how free you are! Now slowly open your eyes. Did you know you're sailing and uplifted right now? What do you suppose I mean?**

Allow time for kids to share their thoughts and ideas, then say: **God has promised that when we put our hope in Him, we'll soar with wings like eagles. As you think about what that means, let's fold flying paper eagles to remind us how God lifts us. Then we'll discover more about what it means to soar with wings like eagles.**

Distribute the paper squares. Then demonstrate the following step-by-step folding directions using the diagrams. Make sure that kids complete each step before moving on. Allow friends to help one another if needed.

1

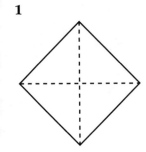

2

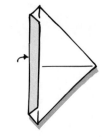

Step 1. Fold a 12-inch square corner to corner, then in half again. Open up the square and place it flat on the table like a diamond.

Step 2. Fold the left corner over to the middle. Then fold the left edge two times toward the center until the fold sits on the center line, then fold it once more on the center line.

Step 3. Fold the bottom point backward to the top point.

Step 4. Fold the front flap forward and the rear flap backward so they stand at right angles to the main body. (These are the eagle's wings.) Pull the flap of paper at the front of the eagle downward a bit to make the eagle's body. Add eyes if you wish. (Fly the eagle by holding the body and throwing it forward. Adjust the wings as needed for better flight.)

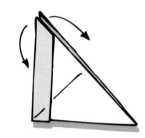

When the paper eagles are folded, show kids how to "fly" their eagles around the room. Bend or curve the wings to launch the eagles and give them a bit more balance. After kids have "flown" their paper eagles several times, have the eagles land in the kids' laps, then say: **Now that you've folded paper eagles and had a chance to make them fly through the air, I have a verse to share with you about eagles' wings. Listen carefully and try to think of what this verse teaches us.** Read aloud Isaiah 40:31, then ask:

+ *What does this verse teach us about hoping in God and His power to help us?*
+ *What do you think it means that when we hope in God, we'll soar on wings like eagles?*
+ *How can trusting in God's help make us feel lighter-than-air and full of hope?*
+ *In what ways does God's help lighten our loads from worries and troubles?*

Say: **This is such an important verse because it teaches us one of the many powerful things hope does for us—when we place our hope in God. Hope placed in God makes us lighter so we feel like soaring eagles. It helps us rise above our troubles just as eagles rise above the earth. It makes us free from worry just as eagles feel free in flight. And hoping in God keeps us fresh, not weary, so we can keep serving God and having faith in His awesome power to help us! The next time you face worries or troubles, close your eyes and imagine an eagle soaring on open wings and know that God is lifting you up and helping you rise above the worries. Place your hope in God!** If there's time, have kids write Isaiah 40:31 on the wings of their paper eagles.

The Great Gardener

Paper flowers remind kids that God provides what we need to grow.

Matthew 6:28-30; John 15:1

Simple Supplies

+ orange and yellow crepe paper
+ scissors
+ tacky craft glue
+ green chenille wires
+ green florist's tape
+ green construction paper (optional)

Before Class

Make several paper daffodils according to the directions. Kids love making these simple flowers that are folded, twisted, and stretched, so plan on having each child make several! Cut out a 2-by-4-inch orange crepe-paper rectangle for each flower. If your kids are young, you may wish to cut out the yellow crepe-paper leaves as well. Provide green construction paper for leaves if desired.

The Fold-n-Hold Message

Gather kids and ask them what kinds of things their parents or other loving caregivers provide for them. Answers might include food, clothing, a home, school supplies, medicine when they're ill, and lots of love! Then ask:

+ ***Do your parents or loving caregivers supply the things you need? Why?***
+ ***Do they always provide all the things you want? Explain.***
+ ***Why is it more important to have our needs met than our wants?***
+ ***How does providing for your needs express your parents' love for you?***
+ ***In what ways does God provide for as a loving parent provides?***
+ ***What are things God provides for us that other people can't provide?***

Say: ***Parents, grandparents, and other loving adults make sure we have all of the things we need. They provide for us because they love us. God loves us and provides for us, too, in every way—even in ways that our parents and families simply can't provide. In fact, God provides for all of His creation down to the smallest details!***

Invite a volunteer to read aloud Matthew 6:28-30, then say: ***You see? God even provides for the flowers in the fields. And if He cares about these smallest parts of His creation, how much more will He provide for us! Let's fold and form paper daffodils to remind us of how much God wants to provide for all we need to grow and flourish! Then we'll discover more about the ways God provides for us.***

Demonstrate the following step-by-step folding directions. Make sure that kids complete each step before moving on. Allow friends to help if needed.

Step 1. Pull the long edge of a 2-by-4-inch piece of orange crepe paper to stretch and frill it.

1

Step 2. Slightly roll the rectangle into a tube, making sure the frilled edge is sticking out. Then fold and twist the straight edge (opposite the frilled one) around a green chenille wire "stem." Wrap green florist's tape around the folded end to hold the center of the flower on the stem.

Step 3. Cut out six petal shapes (4 inches long) from yellow crepe paper and stretch the edges a bit. Fold the petals in half to make a crease down the center of each.

3

Step 4. Open the petals again, then glue them one by one around the base of the flower, covering the florist's tape. (If you would like, attach long, slender construction-paper leaves to the base of the stem using florist's tape.)

When the flowers are folded and assembled, say: **What beautiful flowers you've made. The flowers God makes are beautiful, too, and He cares for them and provides for them. What things does God provide to help the flowers of the field grow and flourish?** Allow time for kids to suggest provisions such as rain, sunshine, and lightning to feed the soil. Then ask:

4

> ✦ *In what ways does God provide for you to grow and flourish?*
> ✦ *Why can we trust God to provide what we need to grow in Him?*
> ✦ *How can we help by using what God supplies in positive ways to help us keep growing in Him?*

Say: **God provides the ways for us to grow, and we can use those ways to help ourselves grow in Him. A flower cannot travel to a river that God provides, but when God provides us His Word, we have the ability to read it. When God provides us with His truth, we have the ability to obey it. And when God provides answers to prayer, we have the ability to seek His answers. Put your flowers in a vase at home and remind your family what God provides for us and why!** Close by offering a prayer thanking God for providing for us and asking Him to help us use His provision in wise ways.

Born for You!

Cool crèche scenes remind kids that Jesus was sent for them to love.

Luke 2:10, 11

The Fold-n-Hold Message

Invite kids to tell about their favorite birthday gifts and why they were so special. Then say: **Birthdays are such fun, aren't they? And I think everyone's favorite part of a birthday is receiving birthday presents. It's also great fun to buy a gift and take it to a birthday person, isn't it? Now think of Jesus' birthday. Who can retell the story of how Jesus was born?**

Allow kids to retell in their own words the Christmas story and how Jesus was born in a lowly manger with only his mother Mary, her husband Joseph, and the animals with them. As you retell the story, use the manger scene you cut out and prepared before class.

When the story is ended, say: **The wise men came later to bring baby Jesus their gifts of gold, frankincense, and myrrh. It was a different kind of birthday, wasn't it? But the most unusual part was God giving a gift to the world when the world never came to bring Jesus their birthday gifts! Think about that for a minute. It would be like you giving your friends and family members gifts on your birthday instead of the other way around. God gave us His Son Jesus as the most wonderful birthday gift we could ever receive! Let's fold manger scenes to help retell this most unusual and awesome of birthdays. Then we'll explore more about the special gift we have in Jesus and why God gave us such a birthday gift so we could be born again!**

Distribute the pattern pages for the manger scene and figures. Lead kids through the following directions. Since the folding steps are all self-explanatory, simply follow the written directions to produce the finished manger scene illustrated on page 51. Make sure that kids complete each step before moving on. Allow friends to help one another if needed.

Step 1. Cut out the manger scene on the solid lines. Cut out the people strips on the solid lines. Color the scene and the figures.

Step 2. Fold on the dotted lines according to the directions on the patterns. When the folds are made, the manger scene will stand up by itself.

Step 3. Fold the dotted lines on each figure so the strip forms an elongated triangle. Tape the ends so the figures will stand up. Embellish the figures and scene using scrap materials if desired.

When the manger scenes and figures are folded and assembled, read aloud Luke 2:10, 11. Then say: **Manger scenes remind us of Jesus' birthday. But do you stop to think about the birthday gift we received when Jesus was born?** Ask:

+ *In what ways was Jesus a gift for all people when He was born?*
+ *How does loving Jesus and accepting His gifts of salvation and forgiveness bring us new life, as if we were born again?*
+ *How, then, is Jesus like our birthday gift from God?*
+ *Who did Jesus come to love as God's gift?*

Say: **All people of all times and places received a special birthday gift from God the moment Jesus was born! He came into the world to love us and to save us. And there can't be any greater gifts than these! Take your manger scene home and retell to your families and friends the story of how Jesus was born—but how *we* received the birthday gift that day! Then remind everyone that Jesus is God's gift of love to all of us and that He is the best birthday gift we'll ever receive for our birthdays or *any* days.**

Close by thanking God for His gift of Jesus. Let kids form small groups and use their manger scenes to retell the story of the first Christmas to one another. If there's extra time, kids might enjoy using stiff, white paper to make additional elongated, stand-up triangles and turn them into the wise men, more shepherds, angels, animals, or even palm trees to go along with their nativity scenes.

Express Yourself!

Fancy heart boxes help kids thank and praise the Lord.

Psalms 23; 100

Simple Supplies

◆ stiff colored paper (a variety of colors)
◆ scissors
◆ pens or fine-tipped markers
◆ copies of the heart-box pattern from page 64

Before Class

Photocopy a heart-box pattern for each person (plus several extras) on stiff, colored card stock or construction paper. Cut, fold, and prepare a box according to the directions. Cut stiff colored paper into 2-by-1/2-inch strips. Cut lots of strips! Kids will write praises on the strips, one strip for every year they are old. You'll also want to send several more strips home with each person.

The Fold-n-Hold Message

Gather kids in a circle and go around the circle as you have each person read a verse from Psalms 23 and 100. If there are more kids than verses, choose another Psalm of praise to read or read the previous two once more.

When everyone has had a turn to read, say: **Wow! There were some awesome praises, thank-yous, and expressions of hope, trust, and love in those psalms, weren't there? Whoever wrote these psalms wanted so very much to express their love and loyalty to God—with words, with music, and with all their hearts!** Ask:

◆ *Why do you think it's important to express ourselves to God?*
◆ *Do our expressions have to be flowery and upbeat all of the time? In other words, can we express things such as fear, anger, and sadness to God? Explain.*
◆ *Why is it especially important and wonderful when we express our thanks, praises, and love?*
◆ *What are ways to express ourselves to God and Jesus?*

Say: **God is wiser than anyone, and He already knows what we think and feel even before we do! God knows us that well—and God loves us that much. But even though God knows how we feel, it's important to express what we're feeling to Him. We want to express our adoration, praises, love, and thanks because God is our Father and because we love Him so greatly. And we want to thank Jesus and tell Him we love Him because of all that Christ has done for us through His teachings, love, and forgiveness. Let's make neat heart boxes as reminders of expressing ourselves to God and to Jesus. Then we'll take some time to express ourselves!**

Hand out the heart-box patterns and scissors. Demonstrate the following step-by-step folding directions using the diagrams. Make sure that kids complete each step before moving on. Allow friends to help each other if needed.

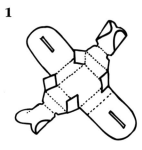

Step 1. Cut the box out on the solid lines (including the two slots). Then pinch the folded hearts together and carefully bring the side of the box upward.

Step 2. Tuck in the side flaps, then slip the two slots over the folded hearts. Push the slots down as far as they'll go.

Step 3. Open the hearts to secure the completed box. You can now open and close the box by sliding the hearts in or out of the slots.

When the heart boxes are folded and finished, have kids read Psalm 100:4, then use markers or pens to write a short praise on the folded heart. After kids have finished writing, hand each person as many paper slips as they are old. (Have kids help cut more paper strips if needed.)

Say: **Think of all the things you can thank and praise God for. Think of all the things you can express your love and thanks for to Jesus. On the slips of paper you have, write a phrase of thanks to the Lord for something specific He has done for you. For example, you might say, "Lord, thank you for helping me when I worry too much. I put my faith in you alone." Or you may write a praise phrase for who God is. For example, you might write, "Lord, you are strong and all-wise. No one is like you, God!" After you write on each slip of paper, place it in your heart box. Then we'll share some praise to the Lord by reading some of your slips aloud!**

Allow time for kids to write, then invite volunteers to pull several of their strips from the heart boxes and read them aloud. After each praise or thank-you, lead kids in shouting or saying "amen." Give kids several extra slips to take home and write on during the week to praise or thank the Lord. Consider having kids bring in their boxes next week to share their praises again.

Envelope Pattern

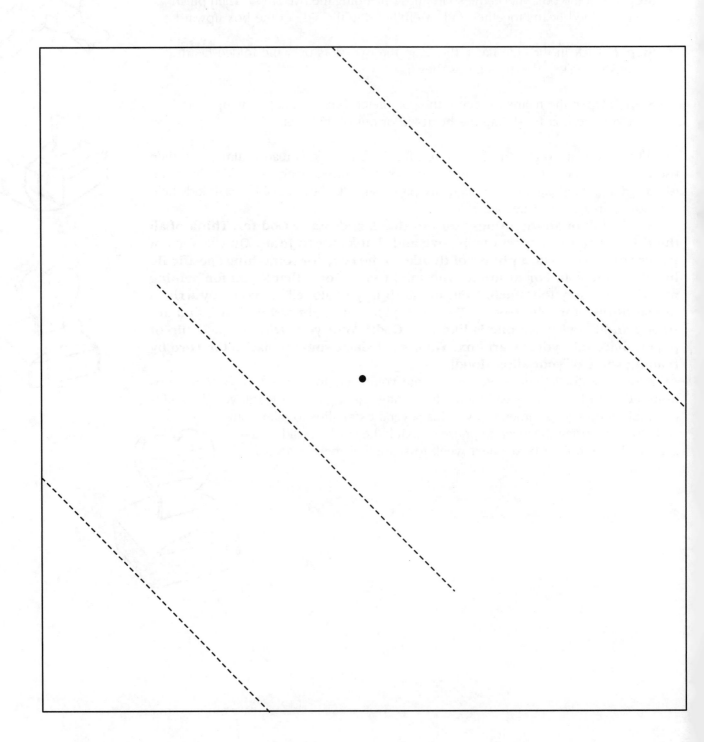

Love From the Cross

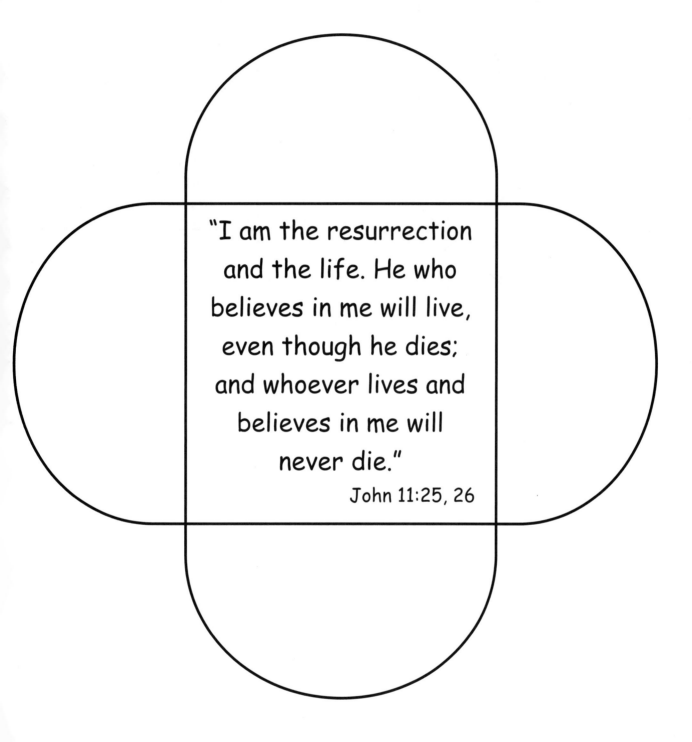

"I am the resurrection
and the life. He who
believes in me will live,
even though he dies;
and whoever lives and
believes in me will
never die."

John 11:25, 26

Dove of Love

"This is love for God: to obey his commands."
1 John 5:3

"Blessed rather are those who hear the word of God and obey it."
Luke 11:28

"Obey the LORD your God and follow his commands."
Deuteronomy 27:10

A Treasure To Measure

Photcopy and enlarge this pattern at 125 percent.

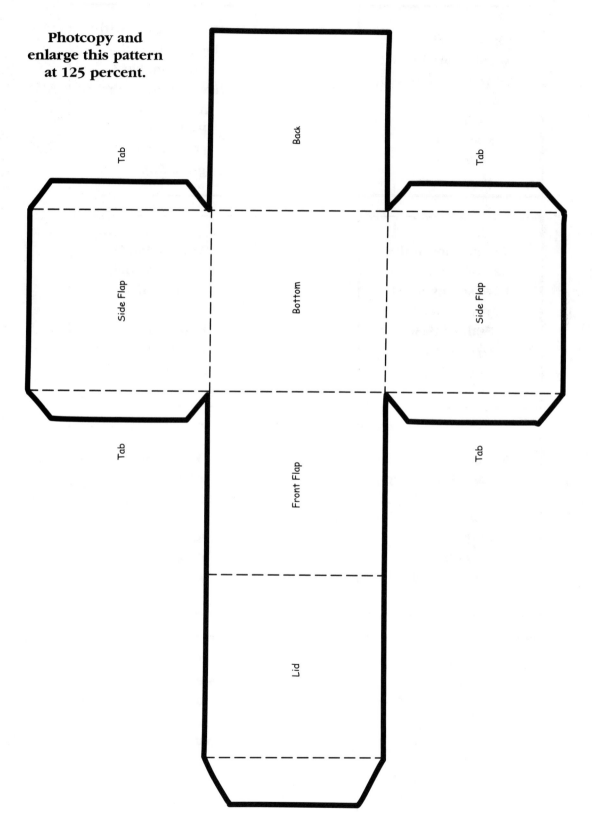

Scripture Cards

"I have hidden your word in my heart that I might not sin against you."
Psalm 119:11
(God's Word saves us.)

"My soul faints with longing for your salvation, but I have put my hope in your word."
Psalm 119:81
(God's Word gives hope.)

"I have chosen the way of the truth; I have set my heart on your laws."
Psalm 119:30
(God's Word is truth.)

"Your word, O LORD, is eternal; it stands firm in the heavens."
Psalm 119:89
(God's Word lasts forever.)

"Give me understanding, and I will keep your law and obey it with all my heart."
Psalm 119:34
(God's Word is to be obeyed.)

"Your word is a lamp to my feet and a light for my path."
Psalm 119:105
(God's Word teaches us.)

"Your hands made me and formed me; give me understanding to learn your commands."
Psalm 119:73
(God helps us learn His Word.)

"Direct my footsteps according to your word; let no sin rule over me."
Psalm 119:133
(God's Word protects us.)

Witness Triangle

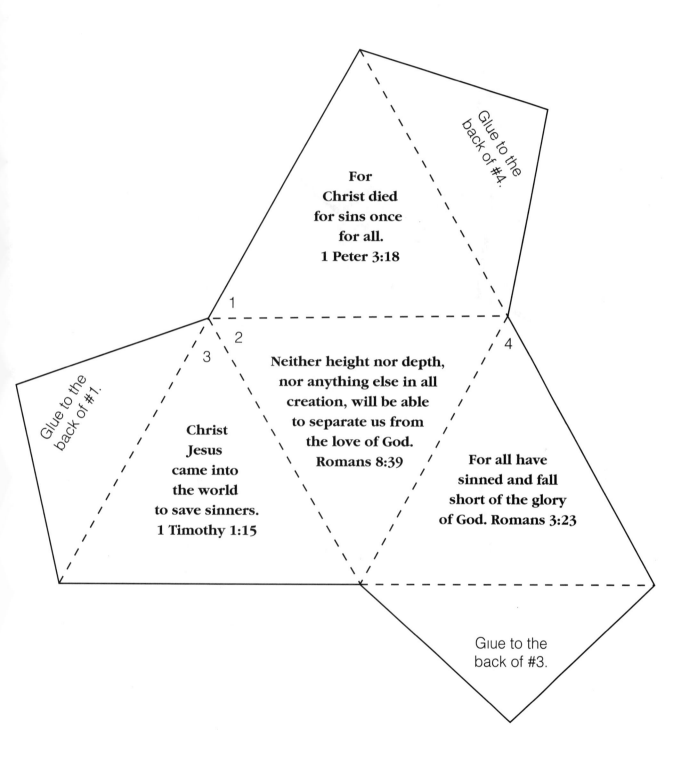

For
Christ died
for sins once
for all.
1 Peter 3:18

Glue to the
back of #4.

Neither height nor depth,
nor anything else in all
creation, will be able
to separate us from
the love of God.
Romans 8:39

Glue to the
back of #1.

Christ
Jesus
came into
the world
to save sinners.
1 Timothy 1:15

For all have
sinned and fall
short of the glory
of God. Romans 3:23

Glue to the
back of #3.

Super-Star Promises

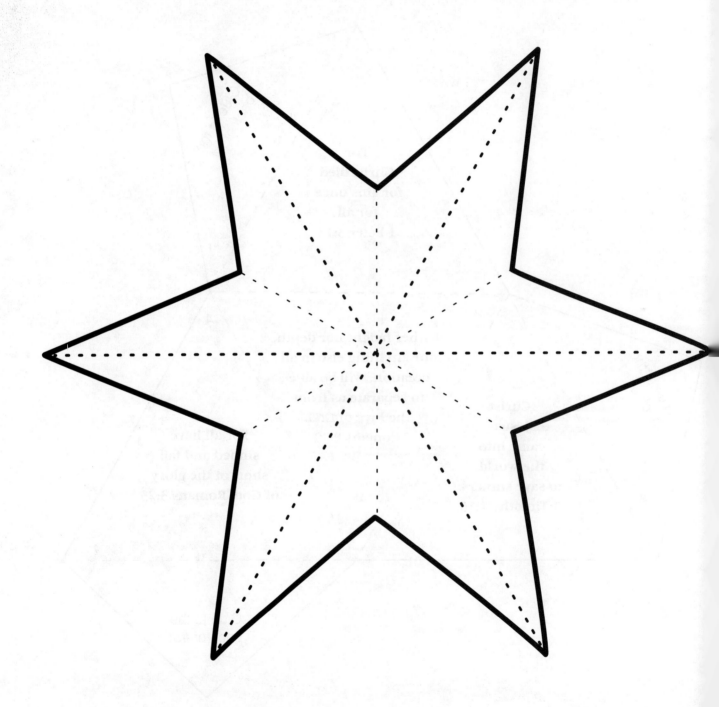

Flip-Flops

Popping Up with Thanks

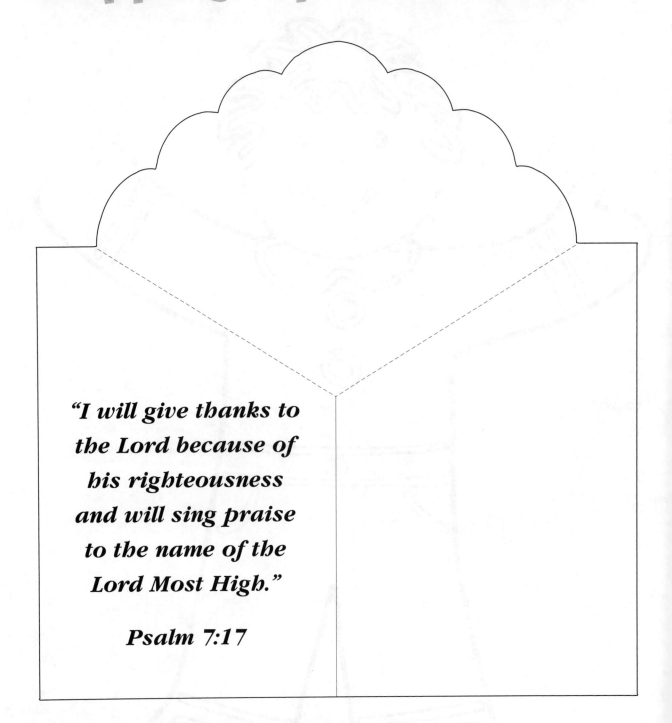

"I will give thanks to the Lord because of his righteousness and will sing praise to the name of the Lord Most High."

Psalm 7:17

Born for You!

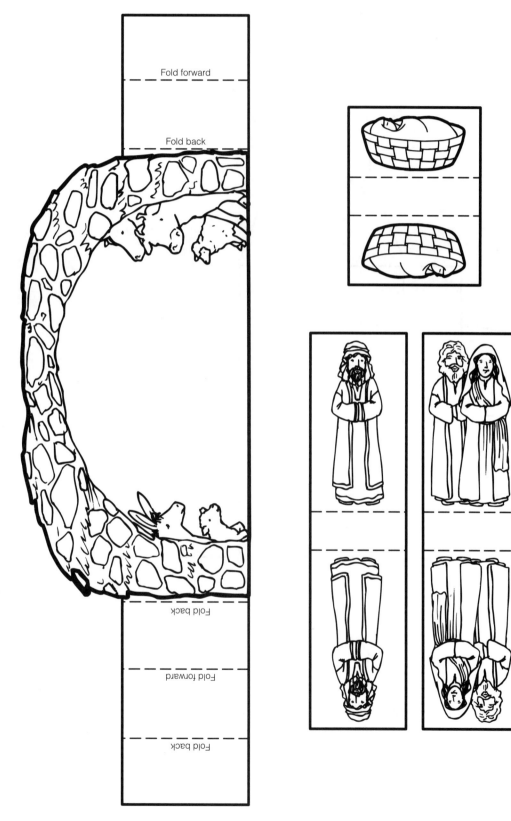

Express Yourself!

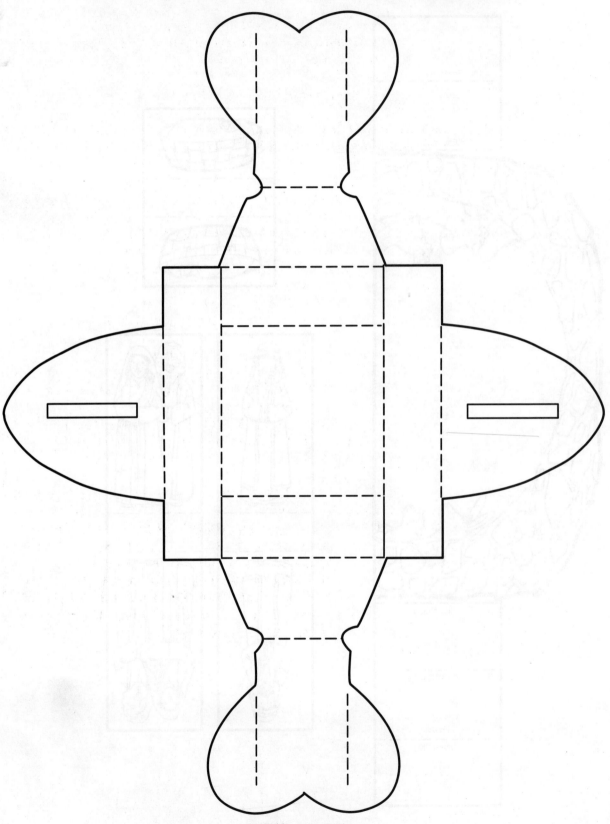